Options Trading

What Can Benefit Your Options Trading Career

(Techniques to Use to Make Profits in a Few Weeks Time Only)

Peter Beran

Published By **Simon Dough**

Peter Beran

All Rights Reserved

Options Trading: What Can Benefit Your Options Trading Career (Techniques to Use to Make Profits in a Few Weeks Time Only)

ISBN 978-1-77485-551-5

No part of this guidebook shall be reproduced in any form without permission in writing from the publisher except in the case of brief quotations embodied in critical articles or reviews.

Legal & Disclaimer

The information contained in this ebook is not designed to replace or take the place of any form of medicine or professional medical advice. The information in this ebook has been provided for educational & entertainment purposes only.

The information contained in this book has been compiled from sources deemed reliable, and it is accurate to the best of the Author's knowledge; however, the Author cannot guarantee its accuracy and validity and cannot be held liable for any errors or omissions. Changes are periodically made to this book. You must consult your doctor or get professional medical advice before using any of the suggested remedies, techniques, or information in this book.

Upon using the information contained in this book, you agree to hold harmless the Author from and against any damages, costs, and expenses, including any legal fees potentially resulting from the application of any of the information provided by this guide. This disclaimer applies to any damages or injury caused by the use and application, whether directly or indirectly, of any advice or information presented, whether for breach of contract, tort, negligence, personal injury, criminal intent, or under any other cause of action.

You agree to accept all risks of using the information presented inside this book. You need to consult a professional medical practitioner in order to ensure you are both able and healthy enough to participate in this program.

Table of contents

Introduction 1

Chapter 1: Market Fundamentals 7

Chapter 2: Brokers And Market Regulations 21

Chapter 3: Trends/Ranges, Support/Resistance And Trends/Range 35

Chapter 4: Management And Mindset 49

Chapter 5: Covered Calls 67

Chapter 6: Understanding The Options Greeks . 78

Chapter 7: Option Strategies For A Price That Is Unchangeable It Is The Iron Condor And Iron Butterfly 102

Chapter 8: Trading Breakout Price By Using Strangles And Straddles 128

Chapter 9: Horizontal Spreads 138

Chapter 10: Straddles And Strangles 144

Chapter 11: Risk Management 151

Chapter 12: Fundamental Analysis 156

Conclusion 181

Introduction

Bonds, stocks derivatives, FX derivatives CFDs, futures, options, ...the list continues on without stopping. The world of finance today is diverse in its nature and there's no limit to the amount of instruments you can utilize to earn a profit. Options are just one instrument that falls within the umbrella of derivatives.

Derivatives are a type of instrument that is so named because they draw their value from a different financial instrument. For instance, futures contracts are a derivative agreement that guarantees a particular value of the stock or financial instrument to be delivered on the date specified in the contract regardless of current market value in the moment of the purchase or at a later date.

Options function in the same method, however there's more in them than an futures agreement and consequently, they greatly lower the risk involved with the majority of trading activities. However there is an important caveat you should be aware of how to utilize options.

Can you make millions of dollars trading options? Sure it's possible. Will you make millions of dollars from this book? It's unlikely. It's true that most beginners dive into trading with hopes of accumulating million of unimaginable riches and approach the entire process with unrealistic expectations.

Trading is a business. If a firm could give its owners one million dollars from only one or two thousand dollars You can bet that the business will ever be in existence since what's the purpose of it? A highly skilled trader, and I'm talking about one of the top around, would anticipate a 20% returns for their money. Warren Buffett has averaged twenty percent from his company since his inception, and is considered to be to be the most successful businessman of all time. So, , if you're expecting 100 percent every month, you'll need to do a fact-check.

The numbers may sound low when your expectations aren't realistic. Trading is a wonderful thing because it's one of the few business where if you be consistent and follow the guidelines I'll provide throughout this publication, wealth and capital will come to you when you have a solid of success.

Your own money isn't the sole way to raise capital. Today there are plenty of capital-sourcing services for traders who are retail, such as fundeseeder, psyquation, or darwinex, which provide an audited, virtual account that institutional investors can look over as well as invest into. Don't get discouraged by the thought that your $1,000 capital won't grow quickly. Be patient and adhere to the rules and capital will come to you, without doubt.

Capital is another major concern for many traders. Just like any other industry trading, it requires an amount of capital to be worth it. Can you now trade with just a thousand dollars in capital? Sure, you can. It is also possible walking between New

York to LA instead of taking a flight in the end. it.

Many traders get focused on the small barrier to entry that trading offers and forget that a low capital investment will cause you to be a burden over time and eventually you'll be spinning your wheels. For the United States, especially, it's not recommended to trade for less than $25,000 and I'll discuss the reasons in later chapters.

If you don't have this amount of capital I suggest not to invest. Make sure you are building up your capital up to the point , and then establishing the proper approach. In terms of mindset, and risk management don't have the same importance in any other book about trading simply because explaining strategies for trading which include the entry points, consumes an enormous amount of time.

This is the thing: establishing strategies to enter is easy. However, managing risk is the most difficult. This is where options can be helpful. They remove all the risks, by defining it from the beginning and all you need to do is keep an eye on the trade. Options strategies, simply will help you get out of your way.

A successful "Options trading" requires understanding the basics first. Fortunately, In this guide, I've provided you a set of strategies that which you can apply to earn profit immediately. To be able to use these strategies effectively however, you'll need to comprehend the concept of risk, and follow the right strategy for trading.

Although entire books could be written about what mindset is required for trading success, I've covered this subject in only one chapter. The book starts with a brief overview of what's happening behind the scenes of the markets, then an overview of risk management and finally mental attitude. After this, it is the only time we'll look at strategies to trade options.

The reason is that the most crucial issues need to be taken care of first. Change your mindset and the profits will come later.

Options aren't an easy fix for your performance in trading, particularly in the event that you are struggling with another instrument. If you're just a beginner Options don't require particular knowledge, but make sure you're protected from adhering to risk and mindset guidelines.

Now, after everything, we'll get deep and tear back the veil to see what happens behind the scenes of the markets.

Chapter 1: Market Fundamentals

We all interact with the markets through financial TV channels , or online via some charts of stocks. Both of these are great sources of information, offer a highly distorted perspective of the market, however. They always bring a sense of panic or excitement, with no other information other than that.

Hollywood isn't helping also. Traders are often shown trading stocks through shouting obscenities at each other and, if the glitzy auto salesman that called his self "The Wolf of Wall Street" is true the use of stimulants and drugs are fairly commonplace.

None of these representations is necessary to achieve success although one could prefer to think of things in this way.

Orders and Traders

Open any trading terminal then the very first thing you'll get is a video game-like layout, with flashing numbers, red or green as well as a variety of lines and graphs indicating which. The lines and light flashes represent only the actions of other traders.

There are many kinds of traders on the market, ranging from traders who don't know their stock from their feet or institutional traders who trade on behalf of a major bank or hedge fund. There are investors and speculators macro investors, high-frequency traders and also traders who are quantitative. The market functions as the solar system that it is, with different strategies and strategies, forming the planets it has.

The sun's equivalent that is the central point of all of it could be "price". The price is the one people are arguing about until an agreement has been reached, you will see the flash of green or red in your display. Price charts show the progression of price over certain time intervals. For instance an a day chart illustrates the price's movement over the whole market session or in the case with FX the entire 24 hours.

Similar to a 15-minute chart, a fifteen-minute one depicts price movements every 15 minutes, and a five-minute chart every five mins. There are a variety of methods to represent price, so let's look at the different ways of representing price.

Price Charts

There are three types of price charts that you can see in the market. The first one is one that gives the most information, and is usually used by the most the most popular media, such as television channels, etc. There may be a connection however it's a simple line chart that shows the price in a straight line changing direction with the percentage change below it, either green or red.

The process of drawing this line is easy enough. Put a dot on the price at which it was closed on the previous day, and then connect it to the dot, which represents the closing price or market close at any given time and you will get a line that is either below, above, or in the same place. This is the way to measure percent change. The line chart looks beautiful and offers easy-to-understand conclusion for laymen. As therefore, you won't see any trader taking a look at prices in such a way.

The second kind of chartthat is a major improvement over the simple line chart is the American bar chart. I'm calling it American because it's usually available in only Stateside and not as much across the globe. The way to represent price in the form of a bar chart can be seen in the figure below.

Figure 1 A bar chart (MetaTrader 4 2015)

Each bar on this picture depicts price action during the specified time period. If these bars were placed on the daily chart, each bar represents the price action throughout the entire day. If the chart is a 60-minute one that represents an hourly price movement and it goes on. Let's look at this in more detail.

The vertical line symbolizes the range of price movements. So, the highest point of this line represents the highest price that price reached during the time span and the bottom is the lowest point in the same period. The higher the vertical line is, the larger the range of price fluctuated. The notch both sides of the line represents the close and open, with the open being on the left and the close at the top.

Bars are amazing in this manner as they don't require specific color or design features. Simply by taking a look at the notch we can determine if the prices increased or decreased. If the right-hand notch is greater then the one left it means that the price has increased, in the event that the one to the left appears more expensive and the price decreases, then the price increased in the interval.

The locations of the close and open notches relative to the high and low give great information regarding the price movements throughout the session. For instance, a close which is much higher than the low and above the high, which is accompanied by an arrow, indicates purchasing pressure that has overpowered selling pressure. This is the same case the case if there is a wick that extends at the top.

Bars, regardless of the quantity of information they offer they do have some flaws. They're, for one, not the most visually appealing. When viewed in a group they seem to blend in with each other. The most reliable method of expressing price movement involves "candlesticks" and that's the method used by most traders who are professional.

Figure 2 Chart of Candlesticks

Candlesticks, also known as candles, as they're known are equipped with the same information like bars do. They provide the close, open high low, as well as the range in which price fluctuated during the time frame. The distinction lies in that the body has an image that is more visual of the price range. Apart from indicating the length that the range is its color will tell the user whether the price dropped or increased in the period.

Bars that are bullish, or ones which have a closing that is more than open are an additional color than those that are bearish, i.e. bars with a close lower than the open. The colors are chosen by the trader. Typically charting platforms assign of red for bearish bars, and blue to bullish bars. This book will signify bullish bars using white bodies, and bearish candles by using black bodies.

Candlesticks give a fast glimpse of the price movement and can be traded in patterns. The highs and lows are symbolized by the wicks that are on the opposite side of the body. Additionally, the dimensions of the body, the size of the wick, as well as its place relative to the body of the candle form an arc that is used in order to make conclusions.

Let's review a few strategies to aid you in getting started quickly.

Candlestick Patterns

The first design that can be extremely beneficial to you will be the inner bar. The example is in figure 3.

Figure 3: Inside bar cluster (MetaTrader 4, 2015)

The pattern is composed by two bars with one on the right being within the that of the one to the left. It's not required that the smaller bar's inner wick to sit fully within the larger bar's body. It's more crucial that the characteristics of order flow of this pattern are recognized.

Inside bars represent a continuation pattern that suggests that the current market conditions will continue to be the case. So when the market is trending upwards and price stalls and creates an inside bar it is likely that the trend you started with will continue. This is the case for the bearish and bullish trend.

The only situation in which you shouldn't be trading is when bars inside are within the ranges. If you're not aware of what ranges and trends are and what they are,

I'll discuss in a future chapter. For the moment, keep in mind in the meantime that bars inside, as well as every price pattern is intended to be used only in certain contexts.

The second pattern that is useful for candlesticks can be found in the pin bar, which is shown in figure 4.

4. Pin bars that are on either side of an bearish bar (MetaTrader 4 2015)

Pin bars are an uni-bar pattern that indicates the reverse. While it's a reversal-like pattern, the best method to trade this pattern for novice traders is to do it using a trends. So, if the price fluctuates in a downwards pattern, once it has taken an extended break within a trend, check for a pin bar to signal the conclusion of the sideways pattern and the resumption in the direction. Figure 5 shows the way this can be done.

Figure 5: Pin bar provides continuation signal (MetaTrader 4, 2015)

A pin bar can be identified by a slim body with an wick or tail that is over or beneath the body. In general, it is preferred to have the length of the tail or wick to be at the least three times that of the body. Do not get too caught with measuring things, but rather be aware of the fundamental trade mechanics.

Wicks and tails are the result of traders denounce a particular price point with a strong. It is more important in the case of a small body since it suggests that the initial upward or downward trend was strong , but was blocked by a larger movement that results in the tail or wick. If a pattern like this occurs near or at the crucial resistance or support level the pattern is almost as clear a signal that the market could ever give you regarding the direction it's likely to be moving in.

"Support and Resistance" is described in detail in a different chapter. However, in case you're not familiar with them, they're basically important levels of order flow where people draw lines through the sand

and defend the line. S/R is an essential knowledge set that you need to master to trade profitably.

The last candlestick pattern which is extremely effective is the "climaxing" pattern. The climax occurs at final point of a bearish or bullish move , and is accompanied by what is best described by the term "exaggerations". The dimensions of the bars are exaggerated beyond the normal size of the direction; the volume of the bars is enormously increased and the rebound from the climax is swift and sharp, too.

Climaxes are trades that counter trend and, generally speaking, I wouldn't suggest beginners trading in this way, but it's actually a straightforward trade to make when you know how to recognize an Climaxe. The reason it's so easy is that you don't have to be concerned about S/R or other market events.

Figure 6: The bear trend comes to an end with high point

Climaxes are often referred to as comprehensive movements. They are identified by huge trend bars that are accompanied by massive volumes. The bars' dimensions and volumes aren't only larger than normal, but much larger, more than twice as large. It is crucial to take note of this extreme exaggeration because it suggests that trend-skeptics are weak that is to say, the ignorant public has made their debut and has jumped on the trend before it's already too late.

What happens next is either a sideways move that ultimately leads to trend reversal or an abrupt counter-trend bounce, which is immediately followed by a meandering, sideways move. This is advantageous , and we'll look at the best way to make trades with these sideways movement when we talk about ranges in the next chapter.

Climaxes are great in terms of the returns they can provide on your time too. With the speed at that prices move against trend post the climax, you'll be earning your profit quickly. From the perspective of the rice environment it is important to be looking for these at the conclusion of trends, and not within the ranges. Climaxes are the cause of zones and aren't present within these.

These are the most important points regarding the fundamentals of market that you have to be aware of and comprehend. The most important lesson to learn from it is the fact that markets are an enormous assortment of orders that match to one another. Furthermore, the orders are a reflection of mood.

It is not always logical but it is often chaotic. But when it is a long enough time the patterns of sentiment emerge that occur more frequently than they do not. If we are able to spot patterns that are similar and identify the inherent risks in these patterns it is possible to trade with confidence. This will be discussed in the chapter on risk management and the mindset.

Remember that you don't require indicators or other tools to trade in the market. They are just made up of price and, therefore the price chart provides all the data you require. The majority of traders rely on indicators due to the complicated nature in the pricing chart frightens them.

Options can alleviate many of the issues however, before we get into the basics of options it is crucial to learn about the most crucial individual in the trading company-- your broker. Furthermore, you'll also have to be aware of the legal aspects of trading and why it's vital to be adequately funded.

This and much more will be included in the next chapter.

Chapter 2: Brokers And Market Regulations

The broker is typically the only one in the market who can be assured to earn any amount of profit. Many novice traders place way too much emphasis on the broker and the tasks they carry out. This doesn't mean that brokers aren't important however, novice traders are more likely to accuse their brokers of problems which are not really the fault of the broker.

The chapter we'll start by looking at brokers as well as price charts. We'll then go over the basics of options quotes on most broking platforms, and finish by addressing the regulation of markets.

Platforms

In the case of brokerage services, there are two options of discount or full-service. Full-service brokers offer end-to- ending options (service options which means, rather than the instruments) to aid in the separation of you from your funds. It may sound like a joke, but it is in fact the normal course of the business of brokerage.

The sole responsibility of a broker is to manage the trades you make. The broker's job is not to provide trading advice or investment recommendations nor is it to give research reviews of the market or provide opinions that will aid your decision-making. Don't make the error of thinking that simply because brokers are an old institution that has a wide range of types of business for example, wealth management solutions and the like, that they are superior to all the others.

In this regard, discount brokers are the best option since they limit their attention to what brokers are supposed to be doing. They do this with reduced commissions and also eliminate some of the more expensive features like having an individual relationship manager, or a hotline that allows clients to call in their trades.

To clarify, I'm certainly not suggesting that you shouldn't put your money into markets of the major banks. If you've got access to an expert financial planner who recommends certain services, you should consider it. My argument to make is that trades are a distinct business and it is not a good idea to consider it a part of an retirement strategy. Instead, you must take profits from trading as a nice reward.

This mindset will eliminate the desire to make money , and it will eliminate a lot of negative emotions that can hinder your trading effort. For instance, double-down on losing trades or not taking profits in the early hours are a clear indication of how you want to earn a few dollars to cover your living expenses by trading.

Trading must be conducted as an enterprise and your broker will behave as a supplier than if you were operating a supermarket store. It is essential to provide a high quality of service, but your costs must be reasonable for you to make into a profit. If a supplier of washing powder starts to tell a grocery store owner what to charge for the product or what margins they should be charging the customer You can be sure that the vendor will be told to stop talking after the fact.

But, many people believe that they will receive the same financial advice from brokers. If you are a trader, you earn more your broker is paid as a result. This conflict of interests is not a problem for a lot of novices. The short and long of this is, select a discount broker, and take your own decisions about trading. Do not seek advice on investing or anything whatsoever of your broker. This puts both of you in an the same position.

In terms of trading options, it is essential to know the fundamentals regarding trading platforms. They include a price chart that is updated in real-time and has the capability to superimpose indicators onto them. Live information on the option chain (I'll describe in detail the meaning of an option chain) and other indicators like open interest as well as market event news and times.

Each broker comes with these essential attributes, so pick the one with the lowest commissions and reasonable rates. It is recommended to use multiple brokers when the size of your account increases to more than fifty thousand dollars. This is to spread your risk more equally. For the moment, sticking with one broker is sufficient.

Price Quotes

When it comes to price quotations You must know three parts three components: the Bid the Ask and the LTP. Let's begin with LTP first. LTP first. LTP is the abbreviation for Last Traded Price. This it is what you see on the tickerboard and in a variety of financial publications. It is the final price that was negotiated and is a reflection of the price of the most recent trade.

Don't fall into the trap of thinking that this is the price of the market. In fact, there isn't a market price, but rather an area within which price changes. This band is referred to as "spread" "spread". Instruments that are heavily traded and have high demand and supply and have a lower spread, and are less liquid. or instruments traded in a thin manner have a wide spread.

Spread is a term used to describe a gap between two points. These two factors are called the bid and ask. When you open your platform for trading, you'll find that the price is displayed in a form of two numbers: the bid and the request. The ask is the amount which is provided to you via the market in the event that you want to purchase the instrument. It is also the amount you will have to pay to purchase it.

The difference between these two is called the spread. It is easy to imagine that the size of the spread doesn't always stay the same. When there is a high level of volatility, which means when there's a huge market or demand that takes place abruptly, causing massive swings in the bid and request, the spread could grow in size, and could even shrink suddenly.

It is usually seen during major announcements of news or other events like announcements of interest rates, and other announcements. The bid and the request will fluctuate up and down by much greater magnitude than they normally do. This is manifested as massive fluctuations and troughs on the price chart, or as larger candles, and gaps between them. Figure 7 shows the concept of a gap.

Figure 7 A gap in the Price bars (MetaTrader 4 2015.) (MetaTrader 4, 2015.)

Whatever the case, the important thing is to keep in mind that LTP is not the most popular market price, but it is an indication of where it was at the time of. Where the spread is currently is dependent on the market's volatility. It could be near the LTP or quite a distance from it. If you are a novice you should stay with instruments that have the lowest volatility as well as high liquidity. or, in other words instruments with low spreads and in which the LTP is typically an accurate reflection of where the spread is.

The prices for options are described similarly and, in general, an option quote includes all the information that you need to know in it.

Options Basics

Option is the type of contract signed between two parties that are a buyer and writer or seller. As we mentioned previously they are derivative contracts and are created from an the underlying stock or FX pair. The person who writes the option is obligated, when writing an option sell an option a buyer, to purchase or sell the stock at a certain price, referred to as"strike cost" or "strike price" at a particular date, referred to as"expiry day" "expiry time".

The buyer is able to choose to exercise the option or not exercise the option prior to it expires. In exchange, the buyer will pay a small sum known as a premium to the option seller or writer. When you examine prices of options for a stock, you'll notice the spread, which indicates the premium price that you can purchase or sell the option. The premium is based on the value of the stock however it isn't the exact.

Options contracts are offered in two forms "Calls" or "Puts". Calls are when the seller agrees to sell the stock in question in exchange for a buyer who pays the strike while a put occurs when the writer agrees to purchase the underlying stock from the buyer. If you buy a call you can purchase stocks at the strike price , and when you purchase put, you are able to offer the share at price of the strike.

For example: Let's imagine that you like the style of AMZN and believe that AMZN will grow in value. In this scenario buying a call that has an expiration date that is close to the current price is a wise investment. If the stock increases in value, the option is likely to be in the money (that is the option will pay you money when you take it up) and you are able to buy AMZN at a lower strike price through exercising the option.

If you are also thinking that AMZN will decrease in value, you invest in put. If it does drop in price, you will offer to sell AMZN at the higher price you strike by taking the put out and buying it back at a lower price in order to earn an income. What happens in the event that AMZN does not move to your advantage, however?

Here's the time to consider options. If your choice isn't in cash when it expires You can give it up. You'll only lose the amount you paid for the option at the time you purchased it. AMZN's current price for shares is at around $1889. If you're looking to purchase 100 shares, it will cost you around $188,900. The 1850 put that expires on August 2nd will cost you only $52.03. Each option contract is equivalent to 100 shares of stock therefore you'd have to pay $5203 for the control of 100 AMZN shares.

Contracts, which include both calls and puts, exist for any combination of prices or expiry date. This means that you can be able to buy a put and call option of $1800 that expires this month, the following month, the month after, and on. Most contracts are not traded i.e. in liquid, with expiry dates two months in advance.

The collection of contracts is known as the options chain. It's simply a list of premiums for each combination of option types (call/put) and expiry date (this month or next month etc.).) and the strike price ($180o $1810, $1790, etc.). As we have mentioned before the moment you exercise an options contract is a way to earn money, it's considered as being in cash. For puts, this occurs when the price of the stock is lower that the price of strike, and for calls, this is where the strike value is lower than the market price.

On your trading platform there is an option labeled "options chain" and it will show an array of strike prices on the specified date for both calls and put.

Market Regulations

The trading of options requires borrowing funds or stocks or stock, sometimes referred to as "margin". If you choose to take a call you're borrowing stocks from someone else. the broker must make arrangements for and you'll need to pay the interest for that borrowing. So it is you must pay interest to the SEC and FINRA as the authorities for the options and stock markets specify that brokers must have the minimum amount of investment for the account that trades.

Now, typically there are 5 levels of risk in the case of options trades , as specified by brokers. The strategies discussed in this book will place you in between the levels one to three, contingent upon the brokerage. At these levels you should be able to anticipate to have a minimum balance of five thousand to 10 thousand dollars.

In addition, you need to deal with the rule that states pattern day trades. Pattern day traders are one who completes at least four trades in 5 business days (Chen 2019, 2019). So, if you purchase or sell 2 options from Monday and Friday, then you're a pattern-day trader. FINRA requires that these accounts should be able to maintain a minimum of twenty-five thousand dollars in balance.

This is the reason I mentioned this number as what the minimal amount you need to have in order to invest in options. But, is it really essential to be able to afford this amount? Can you trade it using lesser? Yes, you can. But, you aren't able to make trades or stop them at your will. Remember that every trade executed counts, and it's not only your trades.

The art of trading isn't a science that says you'll stop trading after one week. It's a mistake and could slow the progress you make. In the previous example this is similar to choosing that you want to take a walk towards LA instead of walking from

New York because you can't afford the cost of a flight. Better to put aside and purchase a ticket instead of to walk the entire distance which could cost you more over the long haul.

There are many experts on the internet who have a wealth of YouTube videos on ways to get around the PDT tag while still trading. What I'll say is that such advice is a sure indication of a scammer. Be careful if you opt to follow them.

We've now looked at the amount of capital you'll require and figured out which regulations apply to you taking a review of some of the fundamentals.

Chapter 3: Trends/Ranges, Support/Resistance And Trends/Range

Contrary to other books about trading and trading, I'm not going go through every technical indicator that is available, and make it appear that they are trading strategies. Why? It's simpler to just examine prices on a chart, and then make your choices in the same way when it comes down in trading option.

It is possible to use indicators however, every indicator that is that is available comes of market and charting techniques and prices. Wouldn't it be more effective to analyze things at the source rather than superimposing some other thing over the top and attempt to draw conclusions? The primary source of data on markets is flow of orders and we can understand order flow by taking a look at the existence of trends and ranges , and then, through the levels of support and resistance.

Trends and Ranges

The price action of the market is classified into two types of states which are ranges and trends. Trends occur those times when markets are heading in a certain direction and ranges occur when the market is moving in a lateral direction. The potential for profit is higher with trends as you could imagine however they can be a challenge for novice traders to trade.

This is due to the fact that the price is always going away from the levels and it is often difficult to pinpoint the perfect entry point. When you think you've found a suitable entry point, it has already risen well above it, or simply hasn't returned to the level you thought it would go to.

This is the reason I suggest that novices study ranges both inside and outside and develop some proficiency in trading them before they can trade. When you trade ranges, you'll establish a profit baseline which will help absorb loss or trades you miss or are liable to incur due to trading trends.

It's fairly easy to identify ranges as we'll discover in the following.

The Range Identification process and the Profit

Figure 8 A Band (MetaTrader 4 2015)

Figure 8 is an example of a classic range. It is evident that, from left to right the price is shifting in a direction that is slanting. A range always has distinct borders at both the bottom and top. In this instance we can clearly discern the peaks that price create from a fairly stable top boundary and a fairly clear one in the middle.

This is the place where the majority of beginners mess themselves up. The price is not going to exactly match in the horizontal direction. In reality, it is almost never able to do this. Therefore, when you try to create zones of resistance and support or boundaries for ranges which are also known as S/R zones in themselves, always search for an area.

In the figure 8 you see four lines: one at the top, and another at the bottom that represent the upper boundary zone and the lower boundary zone. It is important to note that price crosses this zone numerous times towards the top and bottom. But, when we mark the zone, we're more worried about the zones in which the bulk of price action line up and not every single point.

So, as the period progresses, we will have an easy and simple model for making profit. So long as the price is within the boundaries, we'll cut the top off and take a long position off the bottom. Also we could sell the instrument once it is at the upper border and purchase the instrument when it is at the lower border. To earn profit, we could decide to ride the price until the other boundary, or to take the earlier gain.

If you're trading with a directional approach like in the previous paragraph, you'll need to place your stop-loss order outside of the zone. With options, you don't have to worry about this issue. I'll explain later the collar trade that can be used to eliminate any risks in these scenarios which is also a non-directional investment. You can however trade in a direction using options too. You can also purchase put on the highest end of the range, and then buy an option at the lowest.

They typically occur near the end of long trend and before the beginning of a new one. These kinds of ranges tend to be characterized by redistribution within them. In terms of the fact that buyers and sellers trade positions of power within the market. We'll examine the reason for this in the following section.

In either case, you can profitably make trades on the bottom and top of the ranges that occur at the conclusion of trends as well as within them It is more secure trading in the direction that the trend is, using it as an entry level. In the case of a bear trend, trading short at the highest point of the range to prepare for the trend going lower and the trend advancing is an excellent example of entering the trend.

Most of the time, you'll notice an upward trend on a high timeframe, like it's the time frame for the week, and then go in a direction that is a little off. This sideways move, for the lower timeframes typically between five and fifteen minutes, is printed as a range. You can trade it or make use of it as a starting point to get into the trend on a higher timeframe.

No matter what you decide to do, keep far from middle-of-the range because it is where the flow of orders, also known as the presence of traders, is at most and the price flows are uncertain. Always trade in the areas where order flow is at its highest.

Trend Trading

I'll reiterate that you should study to master your trading ranges prior to trading trends. You must be aware of the principles of order flow more deeply before you are capable of trading trends effectively. With regards to trading options, it is not necessary to understand this prior to beginning to earn money, as the strategies I'll demonstrate in the future are neutral to market that is to say you'll earn profits regardless of the direction the market is moving.

Figure 9: An uptrend (MetaTrader 4, 2015)

Figure 9 shows a long bullish trend. Note how the price doesn't increase at a continuous angle, but it moves upwards, down and down in some instances before finally going upwards. They are caused by a set of traders representing one aspect of the market dominating other traders on the market, and driving the price in a specific direction.

When the opposing side moves back, a battle follows, and as a fight it is a sequence of attacks or retreats, as well as defeats. The goal for the two sides to win the market. The more powerful one is, the higher prices will be.

Look to the left side of figure 9 the price is nearly vertical. This is due to the fact that there aren't any sellers and buyers move forward without fear. As the trend advances and the angle that price is moving forward gets smaller until the price turns sideways. then it drops to a low stage where buyers assert their power and raise prices.

If this were an e-book on the directional market, I would explore the ways to improve order flow and to assess how the selling or buying pressure is doing. But when it is about trading options, all you must be able to do is recognize patterns and ranges, particularly the latter. While it's beneficial to improve your abilities and determine the strengths that is the trend at present, it's not required to be able to trade options effectively.

In the end, remember that ranges arise from order flow, where both bears and the bulls are equally strong, and that they both trend from orders in which one side is more powerful than the other.

The most important thing is the ability to draw appropriate levels of resistance and support.

Resistance and Support

"Support as well as Resistance" is often misunderstood in the context of trading. A majority of traders, and sadly even the most advanced ones who ought to be aware, view S/R as a collection of lines on charts. However, the reality is that S/R is the most significant impression of order flow and offers the most effective entry points to the market.

In the best sense, I am referring to starting points with risk at a minimum for the reward. The chance of entering with a solid S/R is minimal because that is the place where you can get the best support from other like-minded traders who can push prices in your direction. Understanding S/R and entering the correct way is essentially determining the motives of the market and then joining the flow of orders that dominate in the appropriate time.

The most important kinds of S/R can be described the following:

1. Highs and lows with swings

2. The areas prior to the chart where price moved in a significant way

3. Dynamic S/R, similar to that of 20EMA and Fibonacci levels

4. Range boundaries.

We've seen before the ways price is able to repeatedly ping away from range boundaries and offer an excellent opportunity to enter. Let's examine the other three options and discover how they operate.

Major and Minor Grades

Figure 10 S/R levels, major and minor (MetaTrader 4 2015)

Figure 10 shows how powerful the S/R entry can prove to be. The image appears a little chaotic at first, but shows the various kinds of S/R levels that you'll be able to see.

From an overall perspective on the market it is an aspect of price action that shows the conclusion of a bear market and a time when orders are distributed, and the beginning of an upward trend. This is on a 4-hour timeframe, which means that each bar is a price movement for four hours. The measure is called that of the FTSE 100 which is the UK market index for stocks.

If you take a look at the horizontal lines that are on top they indicate the highest point level of the range. This range isn't necessarily perfect, but it is valid since as you can see from the circles to the left side, price is being pushed downwards by bears in this area. The bulls won't get them back until later, towards on the left side of the chart.

As the price approaches the high end of the range to the right, it is interesting that the bears do not create any kind of resistance. A trade at this level could have led to losses. But let's see what is to come next. Price crosses the level, creates an elongated pin bar which indicates the continuation of the trend but then dips back to the level in order to make use of it as a an additional support for further gains. We can thus observe that the top of the range acted as resistance at first, but then transformed into support. If you wanted to trade against the trend when that range was broken, previous top of the range would be an ideal entry point.

Similar to the triangles, they show the price dynamics at the lowest point in the price range. Note that the bear trend exhausts itself in the first triangle to the left. Although the retest of that point on the right isn't clean the traders will still be aware of this level and the price utilizes it as a support point to push to the upside.

The two levels above, which are the previous range boundaries are the most important S/R levels in this chart. The more people who hit a level, and the more intense the reaction at that level, the more significant a significance of a level.

When price is moving upwards from the second triangle to left, we see an example of a small resistance zone at one of the squares. The price is pulled back and forms a small swing high in the first square. It then dives and then slams into the swing high using it as a source of support as it climbs.

The price here behaves the same way as it is likely to behave as it breaks through the top of the range. But, the squares are only a minor level, and not a good entry point since currently and the price is within an area. This level is far from the bottom, and orders could be unpredictable. We could have walked down a couple of timeframes and looked for an opportunity, but not in this particular timeframe.

Then, we can notice a Fibonacci indicator near the A letter. Note how the price returns up to 50% mark of the Fibonacci and then goes to the right. This is a minor level with similar reasons to the squares. The price hasn't yet risen over the range, and from a perspective of range this isn't an excellent starting point.

If this occurred in a trend that was strong or shortly after breaking out of its range, this low level could be seen for an opening point.

The point to grasp is that there are levels everywhere, but you should stick to major levels for the majority of the time. You should use smaller levels when the flow of order is dominant in the direction you prefer.

If you've got an understanding of the basic S/R concepts, it's time to examine the management of risk and mentality.

Chapter 4: Management And Mindset

Now we're to the most crucial elements that can make sure your trading is successful controlling risk and being in the proper mindset to guarantee that you succeed. Options are an excellent option to trade precisely due to their capacity to reduce risk more effectively. This is the reason why professionals prefer to use options in more sophisticated strategies.

In this section, we'll explore the fundamentals of risk management, and explore the principles you must have to be successful in the market.

Qualitative and Quantitative

Risk management can be described as both quantitative and qualitative. The quantitative aspect is simpler to comprehend since it's just an issue of crunching numbers and observing the various metrics with regard accounts. In the event that you were trading in a direction and you were trading in a direction, the amount of metrics that you must keep track of is a huge number.

It's a good thing that when you're looking for options there are only a few options to search for a few. Let's look at these.

Risk per Trade

In the end more than anything else, it's your risk in each transaction that will determine the success of your business. It is the norm to never put more than 2 percentage of capital for each trade, and in the case of trading options it is true. The direction of trading demands that you take a lower risk in order to succeed.

The most important thing to judge if you are an experienced trader is how consistently they are when it comes to placing the same amount of money into their accounts on every trade. Many beginners go into a winning streak moments and then play loose and then are victimized by a massive loss that erases the gains they made in the past.

There is an opinion which suggests that putting an amount fixed per trade, in contrast to a percentage fixed, is a better approach. It is important to realize that books could be written on risk management . I'm not sure if I have enough space here to go into the details of statistical reasons the reasons why this is not a good concept. It is enough to say that placing the same amount of money at risk can yield greater profits per trade and increase your winning streaks. However, it can be the same as the losses you suffer.

In addition, because of the exaggerated losses You'll need to make more and more gains to break even, and that will drain your savings pretty quickly since the fundamental math behind everything will be against you. Keep in mind that it is impossible to determine the outcome of the majority of trades ahead of time. Therefore, it's best to take the same risk of your account each time you trade.

Win Percent

The winning percentage of your plan, or the percentage of time you earn money, is only one half of the key indicator of whether you'll earn profit or not. Most of the time, due to the ways we've been raised and had our UR performance evaluated at school, we strive for the highest percentage of wins, thinking that ninety percent is more desirable than forty percent.

In the academic world it is so. But in the chaotic world of markets however, this isn't the truth. Making money from the market is not just about being correct. It is possible to be correct on the market, but lose money in the end. This is best explained when we examine the second part of this equation.

Average Win Percentage

Your win rate is the amount you earn on an average when you actually win in the form of a percent of the account, or as a multiplier of the amount that you risk per trade on an average. If you take a risk of R for each trade which could be the equivalent of 2% from your bank account. And you win 4% on an average win then you'll earn 2R for every win.

The win percentage and the win percentage will determine whether you'll earn profit or lose money. Therefore, out of ten trades in which you win two with a winning rate of 20 and your winnings average is 2R You will not gain profits. This is because your losses of eight cost you 8R while your winnings will be limited to 4R. This is an amount of loss that is 4R.

If you earn 5R in a typical win it will be possible to earn profit with a 20% winning rate. In this scenario the losses add up to 8R, as they did before, but your winnings will amount to 10R, providing you with the overall gain of 2R. If you are willing to risk 2 percent of your account, that is an average profit of 4% in ten trades.

If you can manage to make 200 trades over an entire year, you'll end up making 80% profit in a year. That's exactly the kind of profit professionals make, and requires an incredibly advanced level of ability to be able to reach these figures. My argument is that your success is determined by the combination of both numbers, not one.

As you will see, it's very possible to earn money by being right only a quarter of the times. If you take a standard academic test you'll be guaranteed failing, but in market, it's just one part of the equation.

Strategy Evaluation

This is a great method to determine the effectiveness of strategies. If a method has a low win percentage but a high average win percentage it's perfectly acceptable to apply it rather than look for strategies that have higher win percentages. For instance, if you've used the above-described strategy, and another with 90% success rate, but just having a 0.5R average win rate.

More than two hundred trades, the prior strategy yields 80%, however this strategy is reliable 90 percent of the time will yield 35% on the same amount of trades. Which is the best strategy? One where you suffer more losses, or one that has more wins? It is clear that asking which has the most wins or losses isn't the best way to think about it.

Don't be enticed by high-win rates or strategies which claim that you will not lose even one trade. These strategies aren't available except if you manage an investment fund that is with a focus on HFT front-running strategies where you could have come across this book in error. For all of us it is a matter of evaluating both the winning percentage and the average size of wins in relation to the percentage risk per trade determines the quality of a strategy. is a good one.

Qualitative Risk

Let's suppose you sit to watch a show during the weekend and turn on the television to watch your favorite sporting event. You're prepared and have your TV and other accessories in perfect order. The family and friends have gathered also and all everything, it's a fantastic atmosphere.

There's only one issue the team's top athlete, upon whose performance the outcome of the game is dependent was at the game drunk.

There is a fair amount of these things happening in professional sports However, when they do occur, it's easy to imagine the reaction. The athlete is widely criticized as a buffoonand which is not a bad thing and the sports media can be found discussing the next team he's likely to be traded to in the next. We know that proper preparation is the most important factor to success. Showing into a drunken mess is not an effective way to prepare.

However how many of us actually sit down to trade the moment we've come in from work? We're exhausted and frustrated by everything that's going on in the world, and we think that we could just walk into the market. These same markets are populated with professionals who earn a livelihood from it and are accountable to manage billions and millions.

Do you believe anyone is able to make money trading in this manner? Are you of the opinion that trading is just an issue of learning the correct strategies, and then using them at the touch of an index finger? If so, it's an indication that your perspective isn't right and you aren't aware of what risk management entails.

There is no doubt that you'll need to be prepared and have your mind fully around you when you prepare to make a trade. It is not possible to afford distractions such as checking your phone or trying to figure out a solution at the last second. You require a good night's sleeping and workout and eat healthy.

That's why I deemed the adrenaline-pumping, coked-out environment of the trading floor in films absurd, since it's not possible to trade in this manner. Many beginners are attracted by this 'devil might care' kind of representation and want to do similar things with their own hard-earned cash. It's no surprise that this can lead to a swift loss and the only ones who are willing to get their money are the traders who have put themselves in the position of.

It is essential to adhere to an exact routine for physical and mental health before you can operate in markets. Meditation and other mental relaxation techniques are beneficial and can help you be able to see things clearly in the context they are. Be sure to avoid trading when things aren't working out for you in your everyday life.

There's no law that requires you to trade every each day. Spend time reflecting on your capabilities and to practice them effectively. Make sure that you practice them until you can recall them. The live market isn't an area where you can doubt whether the trade is genuine or not. It is enough to hit the trigger and go for it.

Sometimes in spite of our best intentions we don't always follow through with our strategies. This indicates that the problem isn't as much with our technological strategy or our risk, but more with our mental attitude.

Mindset

This is a fascinating informational point We're not naturally wired to be able to trade effectively. This is the reason that nearly 90% of traders fail within one year of opening their brokerage accounts (Tradecity Trading Academy, 2019,). The positive side is the fact that brains can be becoming machines and we can instruct ourselves to be successful.

The biggest obstacle we have to overcome is our own inbuilt negative bias. The negative bias is part of our survival process that puts more emphasis on negative things us than those that provide us joy. Therefore, you are more likely to keep negative experiences , rather than positive ones.

This is exactly why so many investors chase high-win rate strategies, regardless of the overall profit potential. We've been trained to believe that a higher win rate is the result of avoiding of bad performances that we do not think about the amount we earn per win , on average.

This is the reason why implementing an effective twenty percent win rate system is complicated and requires a skilled level of expertise. A win rate of twenty percent means you will lose eight out of the ten trades. Many people are unable to bear the idea of losing 2 trades in succession, or even being able to keep a straight face and take on fifteen losing trades in the same row (there is an 85% chance that you'll lose fifteen trades in a row when your strategy has a 20 percent winning rate).

The last sentence is likely to convince you that pursuing the less lucrative strategy in the earlier section is a great option, but you are accepting the negative tendency. To be able to trade effectively you must develop an entirely different mental model in regards to trading.

The kind of thinking that supports an extremely high win rate is great in an organized context, such as one in the classroom. In these situations, you have to provide the correct answers and are then the reward. However, the market isn't regulated. It's chaotic. There are way too many participants, too numerous trading systems, and motivations for anyone to understand the whole.

Therefore, you must consider probabilities and odds. Probabilistic thinking is what differentiates the pros from the bogus players. In lieu of becoming a casino you should become the casino. This is a fantastic illustration of how odds work, so let's go around with it.

Casinos are aware of the odds for each and every game that it has on its floors. It is aware that the game X is a game with odds that are sixty percent or, that 60% of the times, the house is winning and the gambler is a loser. Based on this knowledge then, how can the house earn money? In the first place they set the payout according to the size of bet.

The games that offer an enormous jackpot of more than one million, with smaller bets usually have a low chances of winning, with as high as ninety-eight percent against the player. The game is paid for through the number of hands that players play. Even if one player wins the jackpot, it's no matter as the odds will be spread and even in the long run and the house will earn its profit eventually.

It's the reason gamblers are treated to complimentary drinks and rooms. The whole thing is designed to put you feeling relaxed and forget that you're flushing your cash into the drain and increasing the odds against you the more you gamble. Jackpot winners receive instant complimentary rooms and are treated like royalty since it's the best interest of the casino to encourage them to play to improve the profit margins of the casino.

Perhaps, you're noticing the similarities between trading strategies and trades today. What's the point of the outcome of a single trade? The results of a big number of trades are the most important thing because the odds reflect themselves across a larger sample size and not just a tiny one. Therefore, even if are unable to win fifteen transactions in one row, it indicates that you're more likely be successful in the next one as the odds will even with the more time you spend.

So, your primary goal is to maintain the chances and the math behind it. Making changes to your risk percent each trade will skew the math to your favor because the average size of your wins are now biased. Your sole goal should be to keep the odds in line to your calculation and focus on safeguarding your capital. The longer you can keep your capital secure and secure, the more you can gamble and more money you win.

Many of us have negative beliefs regarding money and how to be successful because of deeply embedded programming. Maybe we were poor as children or are prone to a fear of scarcity regarding money. Check out the list below to do a mental audit on yourself and determine how you compare to those with a logical and profitable mindset to trade.

Traders who are successful:

* Know the odds of their system and understand the inside of it

* Are in line with the management of risk

• Push the boundaries in terms of improving their skills

• Follow a well-planned and precise training schedule to improve their abilities

* Recognize their negative the biases and negative beliefs and employ strategies to counter this, for example:

* Meditation

* Visualization

Positive Affirmations

* Breathing Techniques

Are well capitalized and do not look for "get rich quick" shortcuts

* First, practice on paper prior to going live

* Guard the capital of their company at all cost

* Don't dream of yachts or Ferraris following several victories in a row

* Do not think about the despair and the poverty that comes after just a few losses

* Do not require the market to confirm their self-image

* Put their ego aside and observe your discipline as well as risk-management policies

There are many books that help you to overcome the negative thoughts that plague you and change your brain's wiring to be successful. Put your money into yourself and dedicate yourself to your own personal development. The benefits will be evident way beyond the results of your trading.

After having learned the basics, it's time to master strategies for options that have low risk and bring you cash. The success of these strategies depends on the mental preparation you have and dedication to your commitment.

Without further delay we'll get started!

Chapter 5: Covered Calls

The first strategy for trading options we'll examine is called the "Covered Call". It is a long-lasting strategy that is a great introduction option for those who have already been purchasing stocks for investment. To clarify that when I refer to investment, I am referring to holding the stock for a lengthy period of time based on the fundamentals of the stock like earnings projections, revenue, etc.

This type of investment is quite different from speculation . If you plan to implement the covered call on your swing or day trading position trading, it's probably not going to be successful.

Strategy Implementation

The principal goal of the called call covered is lower the price of your stock portfolio. If, for instance, you've bought stock from like Walmart for $80, to fund savings account for retirement, the position is at a good profit. At the time of writing, WMT is trading at $110.62 Let's say that you bought two hundred shares for an of $16,000.

If you could cut down on the initial investment you make in the stocks, also known as the cost basis, then you stand to earn more from this purchase. This is precisely what a covered call is able to do. If you purchase the call option not backed by funds, you get the premium for the option from the contract, which increases your profits. In the end, you make money even while in the position. Let's take this as an illustration.

Key Aspects

Let's use WMT to illustrate our scenario. The market price at the moment is $110.62 and the price you paid was $80. You've purchased 200 shares. Your investment is making an excellent profit You'd prefer to make more money from this.

Covered calls require an accurate estimate of the expected price. The first thing to do is not think about an exact price projection

, but rather to check whether the projection you have chosen is reasonable. If WMT is in a significant upward trend, you'll be required to push the projected price further than the current price if it's in a large price range. If you notice that the counter-trend's participation is getting more prominent and the current trend of WMT is beginning to move downwards, then you should take a chance of a lower than the strike for the option.

Let's suppose we assume that WMT has reached a state that the trend is about to come towards an end. To get a good price for writing the call it is best to select an option that expires minimum two months after the date of expiration. Although this can allow for price volatility for a longer period however, if you're able to discern the market's conditions and anticipate market conditions, you can be able to earn a greater premium.

For instance the call option that expires on August 2 that is one month away at the time of writing, and with an expiration price of $130, has a current price of just one cent. That is, if you wrote this option at this price for the strike, you'd get one cent on it. But, the 20th of September 130 strike call is currently trading at just six cents.

The longer-term option is usually traded for a greater price since it has better likelihood of reaching that price at which the option is struck. This is referred to as the time premium in the price of the option. If holding the option for this length of time is difficult for you, then you can opt for a shorter-term option, however you'll need to select an earlier strike price in order for the same price.

For instance on August 2, the strike call of 125 is available at just four cents. It's not just lower in value , but also has a an even more competitive strike price. The only benefit to consider is that it is more. But, that's countered by the fact that it is higher than the market price.

Many beginners fall into the trap of seeking quick gains and eventually losing their investment due to their zeal and impatience. This is a clear indication that the long-term approach is the better option, as long as our assumption about WMT stopping its upward trend is accurate.

When WMT was in a solid trend that was not showing any signs of slowing down, selecting an expiry date that's farther away, like 150, will work better. You'll pay lower premiums, but your long position will yield a decent return, so it's well worth it. Let's go back to our original hypothesis of WMT end its uptrend, and writing an option that has a strike price of $130. The figures below are calculated on a per-share basis.

Cost of stock purchase = $80

The income from writing a 130 calls= $0.06

If WMT remains at or below 130 until the 20th of September, then our figures are as follows.

Cost of stock purchase = Original cost- Earnings from option premiumsis 80-0.06= 79.40

Earnings earned on investmentsis the sum of premium earned/original cost=0.06/80= 0.07 percent

In the event that market prices stays the same as it currently is $110,

Profit based upon the cost of initial price = 110-80 = $30

Revised profit = 110-79.5= $30.5

If you maintain your stock position for a long time and continue writing covered calls with success and successfully, you'll continue to earn profits from the investment as well as any capital gains resulting from the long position. It's something like having an investment property that appreciates in value, but can also provide you with monthly rental income.

Enhancing Gains and Other Possible Scenarios

The keen-eyed reader will be aware that the yield from investing isn't any. This is only an example, so the strike price was not designed to maximize income. This is an important aspect to be aware of especially for those who are new to the field, because it is about the mindset you should adopt when writing covered call contracts.

The covered call isn't an 'instant-win' strategy. Actually there is nothing in this book that is. The principal goal of a cover call strategy is to increase the value of your long position and to continue to decrease the base cost over time. So, your main goal when using this strategy is to boost your capital gains by generating premium income that accumulates over time.

The most ideal scenario is that your investment is constantly growing in value and because of the consistent increase in premium income, your cost basis decreases until it reaches a level that it's impossible to turn an income since your cost of purchase is very low.

To maximize this strategy to maximize the effectiveness of this strategy, don't implement it until you've made enough gains that aren't realized on your long-term position. In the event of a most unlikely scenario, you'll still be able to make profits. In the worst case scenario, you choosing a strike price which isn't enough from where the market price is pushed over which results in the option being taken through the seller.

In this instance the situation is that you need to liquidate your long position at the strike price , and the account will then be liquidated. If the price continues to rise then you'll be out because you don't be able to hold a position any longer. Many traders who are new to trading are in this position and eventually lose their long positions.

I'll repeat it again that the covered call is an additional income-generating strategy. It's not a main trading strategy. If you look at it this way it is more likely that you will select strike prices on the base of how likely the market will cross the threshold instead of viewing it in terms of return on investment view.

The gains of a long-term position must be considered through an ROI lens rather than the returns of covered calls.

The ideal conditions for deploying this strategy can be found in a fluctuating market either a bearish market or even a moderately bullish one. In extremely bullish markets beware of this because it's difficult for new traders to establish the best strike price.

Are there formulas or method of determining strike prices? There isn't, unfortunately. The best method of determining the best strike prices is to analyze potential resistance levels that are coming up on the chart of prices. If you find an upcoming strike price that is higher than a resistance level to which the price previously responded to, it's likely that it will react and stay at that level for a second time.

So, you only need to be concerned about whether breakouts will occur prior to the expiry date, in contrast to whether it will be able to break out as you would with an trading directional.

Covered calls are a great option from a risk-taking perspective in addition to being a good investment if done correctly. When you are patient and wait for a solid margin of profit to be created for the stock's long position before you write the call, you will be in practically no chance that you'll lose money.

Even if the option is granted, your strike cost is likely to be significantly greater than the cost you paid. Of of course, in the worst case scenario, there's an opportunity cost. However, my idea is that there's no any chance of loss of money if the call is executed correctly.

This concludes our discussion of this type of call. The next step is to take a look at collars that are a great low risk strategy.

Chapter 6: Understanding The Options Greeks

Each option in the stock market has four metrics that go along with it. They are known as the "Greeks" due to the fact that they are designated through Greek letters. If you plan to trade options , you do not need to be aware of the mathematic specifics of how Greeks calculate, however it is important to understand what Greeks are and how they are interpreted to convey their meanings.

These Greeks are the fundamental elements that decide on the future price of options. Remember that when you research the Greeks you're viewing the snapshot. The meanings of Greeks will change as the fundamental values that underlie them alter.

In total the Five "Greeks". They can be searched using any search engine and they will be listed in a straightforward manner in "The Greece". They include delta Theta, theta, rho Gamma, and Vega. In this section, we'll find out what each is and how to utilize them to create better choices in trading.

Delta

The very first Greek is the most crucial of them all, delta. This Greek will give you an idea of how the value of an option is likely to fluctuate in response to changes in the value of the stock in question. In the picture below you can will see what are the Greeks in the case of one Apple call option that has an expiration date of 215 which expires on October 18. Notice this: Delta will be 0.60.

If the share price would rise or fall by one dollar, the cost of this option would increase or decrease by $0.60. The current price of the shares is $217.75 The purchase price for the option is $7.45. If the price of shares rises to $218.10 that's an increase of $0.35 and the price of the option increases by 0.60 times $0.35 which is $0.21 and will eventually reach $7.66. Be aware that this is a per-share price, which means that the option price will increase between $745 and $766. an impressive increase.

One thing you should be aware of is how the delta can change with the passage of time for the choice. If we take a look at the call option of $215 for Apple and comparing various dates. The date is currently September. 22 to provide you with an approximate date. Below is the Delta for the same $215 call, with the dates of expiration:

* Sept. 27: 0.6537

* Oct. 4: 0.6072

* Oct. 18: 0.6

* Jan. 17: 0.58

* Jan. 21 (in 2 years): 0.6474

It is important to note that LEAP (expiring in two years) has an equivalent delta to the option expiring within one week. This means that trading LEAPS beneficial, as LEAPS aren't nearly as affected by the time decay, however they could be impacted by price movements in the stock in question.

Additionally, the option that expires over shorter time frames has a greater delta than options that expire farther out. While ignoring LEAPS, options which expire within a shorter time period will be more affected through Delta. The closer to expiration time the option gets, the greater the delta will increase.

We will now examine the connection between the strike price and the delta. We will therefore stick to one expiration date and for this particular discussion, we will be using the 27th of September expiration date of the Apple option to call. Here is delta for various strike price options:

* $225: 0.1544

* $220: 0.3834

* $215: 0.6000

* $200: 0.9488

The price of the share is $217.75 The calls of $225 or $220 aren't in the money. The $200 and $215 calls are cash-flow positive. The more cash-flow positive options are, the greater its delta it will be. Take note that for a $200 call, the delta is at a minimum of 95 percent. The more cash a call option has and greater the likelihood that it'll follow the price of shares.

In general, as a rule of general application If an option is worth by 10 percent of the share price, then the delta is 0.95 or higher. Therefore, if you're looking to trade options that have an extremely high delta, so that you maximize your gains If you own a company with an average share price of $100 you can buy an option on call with a strike of $90 or less. If a company has 200 shares for a price purchase the call option at an average price of $180 or less and the list goes on.

Options out of the market will be significantly influenced by the rate of time decay as opposed to the price of the shares. This is apparent in Apple options which show that out of money option that has a strike price of $2.25 from the market has the delta of 0.3834 in comparison to the option which is $7.25 in the market has the difference of 0.1544. This is the reason it is more difficult to earn profits trading out of money options when they're very far from the market as in the example above, since in the event that the price increased by $1 , you'd gain just 15 cents per share. However, it's important to realize that you'd still make money and the amount you'd need to put in will be less. Let's look at the profits you'd get by making a one-dollar move in the price of the stock to the cost of buying the option.

Let's first look at the option of $200. The price currently stands at $18.10 This means that you'd pay $1,810 to purchase this option. Should the value of this stock went up by one cent, you'll increase $0.9488 in shares, which is the total gain would be $94.88.

Your ROI is:

$94.88/$1810 100 = 5.24 5 %

Let's now compare this with the $220 call option, which has the same delta, 0.3834. The $220 option for call is just $1.80 which means that the total cost of your investment would be $180. In addition, a one-cent increase in the price of the shares will result in an increase of $38.34.

Your return on investment in this instance is:

$38.34/$180 100 = 21.3 13%

This is a crucial lesson, as it demonstrates that you can earn money with outside of money alternatives. If you read online articles on this subject, they slam on the concept and call it as a "beginner" error. The problem is that the majority of those writing online articles about traders of options are academics who have never trade options. Do you worry about the possibility of a "beginner error" that resulted in 21% return?

You'd have to invest $1810 into one option to earn the profits of $95. What if you purchased 10 options worth $220 instead? You'd earn $383.40 for an investment that's about the same amount.

Be aware of this when deciding which options to choose. Each stock will differ, however for Apple currently, trading in money options can be a costly possibility, however you can make money by trading cash call option and make it much better.

In the event that an offer is in the price of the option or near it, the amount of delta will be in the range of 0.50.

Let's now take a glance at options for put. When you see the delta value of a put it's referred to as a negative number. The reason for this is that the relationship between the put option as well as the cost of the base stock is an inverted relationship that's why to explain it you require an negative symbol. This means that when delta is -0.35 that the cost for the put option would rise by $0.35 one share in the event that it is found that the value of the share falls by one dollar. In contrast, if that price increases by one dollar, the cost of the contract will fall by $0.35 per share.

In other words, the relation between the delta of the stock and price of the stock in question is the same. Think about expiration dates and whether the options are in the money in the money, out of the market or in the money. If the put option is not in the money which means that it's strike value is lower than the share price, the delta will be lower than -0.50 and the further out of the market that the choice is lower the value of the delta.

In the event that the cost of an option is greater than the price of the share this put will remain in money. That means the delta will be greater than -0.50 (larger that is greater negative).

When looking at Apple to find particular examples, a $220 put option is just a bit within the range of the market, and has an average difference of -0.6149. A Put option of $225 which is more in market with a share price of $217.75 The Delta of -0.8356.

Take a look at some of the examples. This put of $215 is a little out of the market. The delta for this put is -0.3420. Puts worth $210 have the value of -0.1666.

Delta in the sense of Probability

Another method to consider delta is that it provides an approximate probability estimate for when the option will expire in cash. If you find an option for call with the delta of 0.84 it could be taken to be an 84% probability that the option will expire in cash. However, if you come across an out-of-the-money option with an average delta of 0.38 which, for example, implies that there just a 30% probability the option you're looking at is going to expire in cash.

The same logic applies to put options, however, you must consider the absolute value or remove any negative signs. If you spot put options with an implied delta of -0.62 this means that there's an 80% chance that the option will expire in cash.

If you're going to look into selling options, rather than making trades on options (that is selling the open option contracts) then this is an important aspect to consider. This is because , as an option contract seller you don't really wish to see them expire in cash, therefore you should sell options with an extremely low likelihood of expiring in cash.

Gamma and how Delta Variables

Gamma is one Greek that is not as well-known However, Gamma describes what Delta changes. Each time the price of the stock that is underpinning it changes or the days until expire change, delta is likely to alter. The amount delta is expected to change as a result of future changes in price is determined by Gamma.

For example, think of an example of a stock that has an average share price of $200 and the strike price is $200 and 20 days left until expiration. In this scenario the gamma will be 0.04. That implies that, if price of the share increases by $1 then the call option will have delta rise by 0.04. The ratio is approximate however, it is possible to observe it rise by 0.05.

Gamma is identical for both put and call options with the exact expiration date and strike price. However, put option have a different relationship to call options when the price of shares rises by one dollar the delta value will decrease to the same amount as the gamma. If the price of shares decreases by one dollar, the delta value for put options will get bigger by around the value of gamma.

If the price of shares for a share was $200 with a put option that has the strike price of $200, gamma would be 0.04 and the delta in the case of the put option would be 0.45. Therefore, we can expect to witness delta rise to -0.49 or something similar when the share price of the stock falls by one dollar. That's exactly what will happen.

The more distance there is between the share price and cost of the strike, the less Gamma decreases. This is because delta will not alter as much when there is a bigger gap. For money options, delta is likely to be near 1.0 thus it will show less variation in the delta value as the price of shares. Out of the money options, you won't notice delta changing as much when there is a change in the price of the share that is underlying.

Let's just keep it as is at the moment, and concentrate on call options for benefit of simplicity. Let's assume that the price of the shares is $200, and we are holding a call option that has an expiration cost of $198. In keeping everything fixed to see the gamma value change and we'll look at the value in 30 or 15 day 10 days and 3 days prior to expiration. When you have 30 days left to expire the delta value is 0.59 and the gamma value is 0.04.

At 15 days from expiration and keeping everything else identical, with the exception of the date to expire of the options, the delta increases to 0.61 and gamma climbs to 0.05. This means it is getting more dependent on changes in price of the stock that is the basis for the option. When the expiration date is 10 days away the delta goes up to 0.63 and gamma climbs again, this time up to 0.06.

Remember that gamma can be the same as an option to put that has identical strike prices and expiration dates.

Let's now move to three days until expiration. The the delta in the case of the put is increased to 0.72. Gamma also increases but this time to 0.10. 0.10.

Delta Valuations for Put as well as the Call

Another fascinating observation is that when you eliminate the negative sign to indicate the delta for an option to put, then the total in deltas for both the call as well as the put at the same expiration date and strike price is 1.0.

Based on the previous example for 3 days prior to expiration , with an option price at $200, and strike of $198. The delta in the case of call options is 0.72 and the delta of the put option would be 0.28. Based on probabilities, we get an estimate of 72% likelihood for the possibility that the call likely to expire in money, while there is only a chance of 28% of the option likely to expire in money. Because they are equal and they have to be in order to calculate a probability, you know what the delta is for the other kind of option with identical expiration and strike rates.

Internal and External Value

Options have a price which is divided in intrinsic and extrinsic values. In essence, intrinsic refers to "inside" (or internal value), and so it's value is due to the value of the option itself which is derived from the asset it is based on. Option value is intrinsically derived by the value of the stock in question and also from its implied volatility which we will discuss in a amount. Extrinsic value refers to "outside" value which is determined by the amount of time remaining until expiration. The shorter time it takes to expire, the lower intrinsic value the option is. The cost of the option can be calculated by adding the intrinsic and extrinsic value. A call option that has the strike cost of $198, and an average cost of 200 cents per share and 30 days to expire is worth $542. The extrinsic value for this option would be $342 as is the intrinsic worth of the choice, which is. The $200 is the result of the difference between value of the option and share price which is $2.

If everything remains the same with respect to 3 days remaining until expiration, the intrinsic value remains at $200. This is because the basic facts haven't changed so in the value of the option that comes from the strike price in relation to the price of shares. However, at this point the extrinsic value is down by a significant amount. The extrinsic value has dropped to just 0.60 (per shares) making a total contribution of $600 to the $260 option price. Be aware that in the money options have intrinsic value , whereas outside of the money options, they have no intrinsic value.

Theta

The third Greek that is interesting is an extremely important Greek known as theta. It is important as it provides an estimation of time decay. Be aware the fact that option values decrease when the expiration date gets closer since there's less time to make the move enough to warrant exercising. This is the real value of the option whether or not it is worth exercising to purchase or sell shares. Even if you're trading options for trading, keep your eyes on the prize.

What theta will try to reveal is that it will inform you of the amount your option will lose upon rollover until the following trading day. Theta is described as a negative value to indicate that the option will lower in value, and it is determined as a per share basis, as is other options related information.

If you see theta listed as -0.10 which means that at the beginning of the day's trading your option will decline to 10 cents per share, resulting in a total value of $10 at the time of market opening. This will happen in the event that you exercise the market opening of your option but it's also possible that other variables will be at the equation. Let's demonstrate this using an example to ensure that we comprehend how this process works.

Let's go back to our illustration of an option having an $198 strike price and an average share price of $200. Let's look at both put and call options to determine how this plays out. Theta will be identical for both the call and put options, however it will not be exactly the identical. In this instance, for the call option, theta will be -0.12. That means the call option will decrease in value by $12 by market opening. If you choose to put the option, it would drop around the same amount. Theta in this case is -0.118.

The call option on our hypothetical closing of the market with 10 days to expire is priced at $363 and has an intrinsic value of $163. The price loss total is the extrinsic value. Therefore, that at the opening of the market the following day, the value of the extrinsic for the option will fall to $151, as the ta value is -0.12.

The put option also has the same value extrinsic, which is $1.62 per-share basis.

Therefore, we anticipate it to fall to $1.50 the following morning. It is important to note that as the put option is out of money and has no intrinsic value.

When the roll-over occurs in the next morning, the cost of the options falls according to the plan. The call option decreases to $351 for the entire cost. It is expected that the extrinsic value is now $151. It is impossible to change this , it's going to keep falling with every passing day , and it does not matter what happens to other aspects of the choice.

Does that mean the option is a loss-making bet? Absolutely not - changing shares prices can affect the cost of the option much more than the time decay. In this scenario, the delta of a call option is 0.64f and for each one cent increase in price of shares, the value of the option is likely to increase by about $64. If the price of the share would rise to $201 and the call option was to be exercised, it would increase in value to $418. We've lost $12 in extraneous value, however the increasing price of the share means we've earned a net gain of $55. The put option reduces price to $117 in this case.

Then let's go back to bring the price of the share back to $200 and see what happens as a consequence of time decay for an option called a put. The cost that the put options cost decreased from $162 to $150 , as anticipated from the theta price. This means that when the price of shares rises to $201 following market opening the put option is reduced further, to the $117 value that we discussed earlier. However, if the share price fell to $198 the put option could actually appreciate substantially, reaching $235. In that scenario, you would erase the value that was lost because of time decay.

The purpose for this activity is realize that each day, when the market opens options lose some value because of time decay. However, markets aren't static , and even small fluctuations in the price of shares can more than compensate for the losses that are associated with time decay. It's therefore not necessary to be panicking in the event of worrying about time decay or when you notice your options dropping in value in the first few minutes when the market is open. At the time the market closes, things may be different. The time decay happens only every once in a while when markets are open.

Vega

Vega is an "Greek" which is linked to the changes of implied volatility. You can see this by looking at any chart of stocks price, stocks are "volatile" that is to say that they fluctuate a lot. The curves of the stock market aren't smooth, they're sharp as prices move between up and down. The up and down motion is often referred to as volatility. And the more unpredictable price swings, the more volatile the stock.

The volatility of the market has an an effect on the price of options. Keep in mind what we talked about in relation to time decay. Options have greater intrinsic value when there is more time prior to expiration of the option because it allows the stock to have more opportunities to move move in a way that the option is gaining value since for an option to call, the price of the shares could move over the price of strike or in the case of a put option, it gives the opportunity for the price of shares to fall below that of the strike.

The more volatility you experience, the greater value for options and vice versa. The higher the level of volatility and the greater the price swings the stock experiences. This means that there's a higher chance that the price will to fluctuate in a manner to value the option more. It could even be worth more over a short duration, but that can be an opportunity to make more profit.

Implied volatility is a less than volatility. It is possible to look up any stock to determine its volatility in relation with the average market. This can be done by examining beta. If beta is less than 1.0 The stock is in the middle of volatility. If beta is higher than 1.0 is then the stock is more volatile than the average. An average volatility of 1.72 implies it is 72 percent more volatile than average of the market. If beta is lower than 1.0 means that the stock is more stable as compared to the stock market's average.

The volatility of the market isn't something that can be not fixed. It increases as you approach the date of an earnings conference such as. For options, the most important idea is implied volatility, which refers to the volatility likely to occur in the near future. In addition, higher implied volatility can cause options prices increase. If volatility is less, the price of options will fall. When you are getting closer to an earnings call, which could cause stocks to move aggressively either in one direction, or the other implied volatility can rise in large amounts, causing the price of options to rise by significant amounts.

If the volatility exceeds 19 percent, the the vega is 0.124. This gives us an approximate idea of how the option price would change if volatility increases or decreases by one point. If we consider a strike price that is $95 on an company with a 100 cents per share as the price. With 14 days until expiration and an average volatility of 14 percent, a call will cost $504. Vega can be 0.013. An increase of 2 points in volatility could result in the option price to increase to $508. If the volatility increased by 20%, then the price would go up to $518. Vega alters as volatility increases and it could rise to 0.032. This means that the more volatility increases in the future, the more receptive the price of an option is to changes in the volatility. Volatility has less impact on the pricing of options as the changes in the underlying value of the asset, but in close events such as earnings calls, volatility can be quite high and is a crucial aspect. In our case, if the volatility increased up to 40%, the price of the option would increase to $631.

Rho

The last "Greek" can be described as Rho and is closely related to the interest rate. If interest rates increase the impact is on options prices, however the effect isn't that significant. Rho offers an estimation of the effect of a 1percent rise on interest rates. This is expressed as a "risk-free rate" that is linked to 10-year US Treasuries.

Chapter 7: Option Strategies For A Price That Is Unchangeable It Is The Iron Condor And Iron Butterfly

The main focus on the initial treatment of options is on purchasing puts or calls to profit from the rising or falling prices of stocks. But, these types of trades on options suffer from one of the biggest weaknesses - being unable to determine the direction of price movements.

It is, of course, possible within a reasonable range. It is possible to learn topics such as technical analysis and chart signals, as well as candles, and trending charts to come up with fairly accurate estimates of price movements for stocks. But this is a risky, in that you're just as likely to fall short as you are correct in a lot of cases. There are a few options traders who deal in straight call options, however, the majority of professional options traders don't approach markets this way.

It's because although you may be able to find gold however, it's not easy to achieve it every day the day and out. The most problematic part of this equation is in predicting the direction that a price change. But what if we look at options trading in an entirely new approach, in a different way and instead of doing this, we eliminate the directional fluctuations completely? There are several various strategies that can be employed in this regard.

There are many other scenarios that can occur in the market for stocks. After earnings calls the stock may be able to move either high or low in large amounts in a single direction. As you've probably guessed, it is largely based on whether the earnings "beat" or are not able to meet expectations. To be truthful, this seems quite ridiculous. If an analysis believes that an amount of profit will be realized during a particular quarter, however, the business has a profit, but not as much than what was anticipated it is regarded as to be a significant "disappointment" and can cause stock prices to fall by a significant amount. If the business happens to exceed these imagined expectations, then the stock price could go up.

However, at other times the stock will be stuck within a certain variety of prices. This could be the case for lengthy period of time. The range could be limited, so it is difficult to make money trading put and call options when the market is in this type of pattern. However, the capability to combine calls and put together allows us to develop strategies that earn money in surprising ways. We'll take the chance to look at the various schemes within this section.

The Iron Condor

The first type of trading that we will explore is the iron condor. This is the type of trade you should to use when the lows and highs of prices for stocks appear to be in a bind. It's as if the price of the stock is in a trap. It does not break above a particular price level, which is known as resistance. However, it does not fall below a certain price level that is known as the support. Sometimes, stocks can remain by this kind of structure for a lengthy period of time. It could look like this:

For the support or resistance you need, you'll need to be able to see your price touch the support line at least twice and the resistance line at least twice. The price difference could be quite minimal. There are a few options for trading put and calls. If the price falls to support You can purchase call options and earn profits when the price moves back upwards towards the resistance price level. After that, you can purchase put options and then sell them when they drop back to support.

However, there is another method to profit from this type of price trap. I prefer to call it. This kind of trade is known as the iron condor. In the world of options traders who want to earn a living iron condors are among the top well-known options to trade. If you have it set up correctly, you could make recurring income.

Let's have a moment to make an important note before we explain how to set up your trade. There are two types of traders who trade options. One kind of options trader is one who is a profit-seeking trader. Naturally, all traders want to make money, but an investor who is profit-seeking is one who bets on the direction that the stock will do, and then they play the dice in hopes of making a profit.

Another type of options trader is one who trades income. This kind of option trader is looking to limit the risk and also set up trades in order to earn regular income from market. There are numerous methods to achieve this, and the majority of the methods involve selling rather than buying options. If you're a regular option trader, you buy to begin your position. Therefore, you'll be managing your business by purchasing low and selling high to earn profit.

A trader who earns income sells to open positions. They aim to make money by selling options. While you've been worried about theta and time decay as an income trader, you really value time decay and don't want to wait until options expire.

Iron condors are the very first strategy we're going to examine which works this way. If you decide to trade with an iron condor you're going to trade it in order in order to open your account. You will then profit from the time decay. If the price stays within the range you define as your iron condor you'll gain profits. If it is outside the limits that the condor uses to define then you'll lose cash.

So let's take a look at its is set up. The purpose of iron condors is to establish boundaries on the price of the stock, so we will be looking for a range price for the stock as seen by the chart above. To determine the upper bounds, we're going to make use of call options. The lower bounds of this range will be determined making use of put options.

One iron condor isn't likely bring you a massive quantity of funds. The fundamental premise behind this is that it is a risk-free, trading strategy that is limited in profit. It is not necessary to speculate which direction the price will be moving Instead, we will only determine the limits of price movements throughout the life that the choice is in. In normal circumstances, this kind of bet will perform in the majority of cases. However it is possible that there will be unexpected news, like the news of a negative outcome for the business, it could lead to prices moving out of the boundaries of iron condor and make the bet into a loss. In the event of unexpectedly negative news regarding the economy or the political climate could have the same effect.

We can also discuss volatility. If you remember from the previous chapter that when volatility is high, this means that stock prices fluctuate between high lows and high. We are trying to find an environment where stocks are essentially bound within an extremely narrow price range which means iron condors are one type of investment that you should consider using in times of low volatility.

To make Iron Condors, we're planning to exchange four options simultaneously. We'll trade two options, and purchase two options. Let's first look at the highest price range to trade. In the beginning, we'll want to offer an option to call with an less expensive strike. The strike price that is used to sell the call option determines the upper limit for the condor made of iron. This means that you set this up on the assumption that the price of the stock will not be higher than what the price for the option you have selected.

The second step is purchase an option to call that has an increased strike cost than the previous call option. This is because we will make use of it to mitigate our risk. Let's take a look at how this could perform. In our case we'll assume that the price of stock is $200.

It is possible to offer a call option that has the strike price of $205. This implies that we have set up our iron condor on the assumption that from now to the expiration date and the price of the stock isn't going to go above $205. If there are only 30 days until expiration and volatility is moderate 15% the cost that a call options that has an expiration date of $205 will be $1.55.

The breakeven value is calculated when you add the value of the call the price of strike, and this will yield $206.55. So long as the price of shares remains at $206.55 or less the price, it's not worthwhile to allow an option that can be used. If, however, the share price rises over that amount it is possible to have the option exercised. If you have an option to call, you are the option seller it means that the option seller must offer 100 shares for the rate of $205 per share.

What is the procedure in real life? The way it is actually done is that your broker purchases the shares at market prices and then sells them to the counterparty under the option contract, thereby closing the deal at the less expensive strike rate, they impose loss. If the price of the shares was $208, you'd be losing $3 per share, which is the total loss would be $300 per contract, which could be enough to cover 100 shares stock.

Naturally, stock prices can climb to any price at the very least. This means that you could get in real trouble if your price of the stock jumped much higher. The iron condor can limit maximum losses by adding an additional call option with a greater strike price. You purchase this call option that means you are limiting potential profits due to this additional expense. In addition to limiting potential profit, it also limit losses.

Because you're purchasing the option with a call and you wish to exercise the rights of the option to purchase stocks at the strike price. You can then sell at a higher price to cover any loss.

Based on our price setting that we have created, we can select an amount of $210 to be the price for our second strike. If the price of the stock goes up to $212. In this case the first option with the $205 strike price likely for exercise. Therefore, we must purchase shares for $212 and offer them for sale to the counterparty to the $205 option for $205 per share, which is an overall loss of $7 per share.

However, we are now able to take advantage of the second call option we purchased. In this scenario we purchase shares of stock for $210, and then sell them on the open market for $212, resulting in an average of $2 per share.

This can help reduce the overall losses, and reduces the loss to $5 per share, which is a loss total of $500. The loss is not capped. It's the difference between two strike prices that we choose to be our choices.

Let's now turn our attention towards the other part of the deal. This time, we'll have two options for putting. We first establish the lower boundary of the iron condor, by selling an option to put. You can set it to any amount we like however, to get an iron condor that is symmetrical, we'll choose an amount of $195 as the strike price. A 10-dollar range is an excellent one to choose in the iron condor. The chance of the price exceeding a certain 10-dollar range is very low, as long as you've chosen the right low volatility scenario.

The options you offer are the ones that define the boundaries of an iron condor. In this instance we have the call option, which has an expiration date of $205 as well as an option for a put with an expiration date of $195. This means that as long as the price of the stock remains within the range of $195 to $205, between the date we sell to open the position and the time when our options run out, then we gain profits.

As well as selling a put option we'll try to reduce risk the same way as we did with the setup of call options. This means that we're planning to purchase put options that has a lower strike value in order to determine the lower limit for an iron condor. It could be any amount, but for clarity, we'll set that at the distance of $5.

Let's take a look at what could occur if the price of the stock was to move outside of the range that we've created towards the downside. We bought a put option with an expiration date of $195. We also purchased an option to put with a strike of $190. If the price of shares of the stock drops below $195, but stays above $190 the put option we sold allowed to be exercised. If a put option gets exercised , we are required to purchase shares of stock at the price of the strike. This means that we need to purchase shares for $195 a share, even though the price in the market is in between $190-$195. suppose to illustrate, that it's $192. Then we have to sell shares at market price. Therefore, if we sell shares at $192, we lose $3 a share. This is a loss of $3.

If the price of the stock continued falling, we'd be faced with increasing losses. That's why we invest in the second put option. it has the same function similar to the first call for reducing the losses. If the price of the shares is dropped to $170, our losses would be limited to the difference between strike values of 2 put options. Instead of having to buy the shares back at a current market value of $170 per share, we'd be in a position to take advantage of the second option and sell the shares for $190 per share. Therefore, we would have to purchase shares at $195 each even considering it was market value of $170 per share. But then we could sell them to a third party at $190 per share.

I've simplified the topic slightly, as you must include the net cost of taking the positions. Because you earn credit for registering an iron condor and you can sell it open - this reduces the risk further. Let's look at what the costs are for each option for this scenario:

$$ $210 Call Option (BUY): $0.57

* Call Option: $205 (SELL): $1.55

* Put Option $195 (SELL): $1.45

* $190 Put Option (BUY): $0.47

The price of purchasing one of the options costs $0.57 and $0.47 which is $1.04. However, we get credit when we sell the other two options at $1.55 plus $1.45 which is $3. Our credit net is $3-$1.04 equals $1.96.

We begin out ahead by $1.96. If we do end up losing the trade because the stock fails in some way or the other the losses that were already set at $5 are diminished by this sum, therefore our total potential loss in any scenario is $5 ($1.96 x $1.96 is $3.04. The maximum loss is $304. (for the

100 shares) and the maximum profit that is guaranteed is $196. This kind of scenario is illustrated in an iron condor graph

The example above shows an iron condor, with an inner strike of $40 and $50 , for an lower-priced stock with a maximum profit of $100 and a maximum loss $400.

In the two instances we've looked at so far, the losses appear to be greater than the gains. This is, however, an untrue way of looking into the market. When you have an iron condor, your odds of winning the trade, if you've done your research and selected a stock that is that is low-risk is high. This means your chance of winning is very high. The secret to success with Iron condors is to take your time selecting your trades and studying them. Don't pick a random company and then join your iron condor.

If the condor is within the range you set the options are likely to lose value due to time decay as days go by since all the options will be worthless. This is why iron condor traders usually declare that they earn profit by utilizing time decay.

Buy Back to Close

Another strategy is to purchase another iron condor in order to end the transaction. You have the option of doing the same or do not. The reason to consider doing it is the possibility of the stock breaking either way or another, and you'd then be placed in the situation where the options you sold granted. The counterparty of the transaction will have the option to either buy or sell securities. If you sell an option, and it's exercised, you declare that you've been given the option.

If you're assigned, you're required to fulfill the conditions of the contract. However, it is all automatic when you make these kinds of trades. The broker will manage the task for you and you don't be aware of what's happening except for the losses appear on your account.

It is possible to trade iron condors in various time frames. The longer your time period, the longer you'll need to wait for or for time decay to perform efficiently enough to let you purchase it again and earn a profit or let it expire to make the highest profits.

In the event that you opt to purchase the item back earlier, you could still earn an income, but it'll make less money than what you could have earned. The more time you have before the date of expiration, the more favorable. If the price of the stock remains within the price limits, and there's not any indication of it being likely to break out in one direction or another the chances are fairly safe to let the condor's iron expire. Some traders would rather be safe and purchase it back in the few days remaining. In that time, rate of decay has cut the value that the trades are traded at, therefore purchasing them back isn't likely to impact your profits as much.

Assignment could occur anytime, but it is most likely occur when options expire. A lot of people are misled by assertions like "most options expire and are worthless". It is true that when you have money options that you've purchased, and are permitted to expire, they'll be exercised. Any money option which expire are automatically exercised from the brokerage. If you make trading like an iron condor, the losses are absorbed. Also, it is best to have sufficient money in your account to cover losses.

If you're close to expiration , and there's a breakout either or the other way Instead of waiting for the contract to expire, you can buy the contracts back. It is likely to result in loss in this scenario However, it's more beneficial to limit losses than let the options expire , and end up in an even more dire situation. The idea is to buy them back earlier is likely to require the purchase of them again, which means making some losses however, you should avoid getting the options exercised.

Iron Condor: Summary

Thus, an iron condor can be an investment type that is worth pursuing when you are convinced that the stock in question will not experience significant price changes between the time you open the account and the date that expires for the options. Though we've covered the four options necessary to establish an iron condor, as if they were separate trades, it is possible to enter an iron condor as one trade. Each option will share the same expiration dates, but they'll have distinct strike prices, as explained. You can set up an iron condor on any time period you prefer, but professionals prefer to opt with a 30 or 45 day timeframe prior to expiration.

The highest profit from this condor determined through the credit you receive upon opening the position. This is the money you get for selling the two options using the prices of the inner strike less the cost you pay to purchase options at those with the outside strike price. The inner strikes define the price limits of the condor iron. You will lose money when the price of the shares goes beyond the limits established by the inner strike at the time of expiration.

The possibility of losses has to be assessed on each side of the transaction. In our case we set up an iron condor which was symmetric , so the potential losses were identical. For every side of the transaction, the highest losses is equal to the sum of the outside strike value and internal strike price, minus the net credit from selling the condor.

There are trade-offs to be considered when the process of setting up iron condors. It is possible to increase the chance of earning money, however this can reduce the amount of earnings you could make. Riskier means that you are able to make more money. A higher risk situation is one where the range created between the strikes that are inside is smaller. However, you could increase your profits by choosing larger ranges between the outer and the inner strike prices. If the trade proves to be a losing one and you end up losing more money.

In the majority of cases iron condors are likely to suffer losses that are greater than the maximum amount of profit they can earn. However, losses are capped so the chance of profit will be higher.

The method used by the majority of iron condor trader is entering trades that have lower profits with a higher chance of earning profits, and then to make up for the losses with a greater quantity of trades. If you're earning $200 per trade and you want to earn $5,000 per month from iron condors, then you can simply enter into 25 trades in a month.

There are many instances of a specific trade if you feel that it is likely to have a high chance of success, however it is recommended to use diversification strategies in your trading. Like trading put and call options iron condors, trading them will come with a possibility of failure and you're likely lose on a few or all of your trades.

Iron Butterfly

Iron butterflies are another kind of trade that has four choices. In this case, you're trying to reach a certain share price to increase profits However, the trade may also be designed with the possibility of a directional bias in one direction and the opposite. For the iron butterfly we alter the iron condor through selling call and put options at exactly the same price.

For the example of the iron condor we traded put and call options at the inner strike price of $205 and $195 respectively. We then purchased the put and call options with strike prices of $190 and $210 respectively. The strategy made money by ensuring that the stock would remain the range of inner strike prices. This is in the range of $195 to 205.

In the event of the iron butterfly scenario, we'd create the trade according to. We would offer the call option at the strike price of $200 and then sell put options that has a strike price of $200 and each with the exact expiration dates. We could then create an option range by purchasing an option for $195, and then buying an option to call that has a strike price of $205.

The goal of this iron butterfly will be that the price remains at or around $200. This would give us the most profit. We can close the position earlier if needed similar to Iron Butterfly.

The net credits you receive for an iron butterfly is the premiums you earn to sell the call and put at the middle strike price, less costs for purchasing the put and call options.

A maximum amount of loss expected to be the greater of or the greater of both the price of the middle and lower price less the amount received in credit as well as the distinction between top strike price and middle strike price, less the credit that was received.

In our instance we have made it to be symmetrical, so we could calculate the middle strike cost plus what the strike cost is for the put option, which is $200-$195 = $5 before subtracting the credit. If we had an option with a strike price of $200 and the credit in the amount of $6.87 for each share. The put of $195 will cost $1.45 while the $205 call will cost $1.55 So the net credit would be ($6.87 + $1.45 and $1.55) 100 x $387. This is the highest possible profit , assuming the price of shares remained close to $200.

An illustration depicting an iron butterfly taken from the guide to options on Wikipedia is presented below.

Summary: Profits from Stock Aren't Moving

Iron condors are more than a popular trading strategy due to the fact that the iron butterfly rely on the stock to remain at the same level in comparison to the iron condor, which offers the stock an area that it can be able to move around within. A condor with an iron symbol is a great method that you can use to earn regular income. A lot of traders trade only with iron condors. However, you could also mix the trading of iron condors with other strategies to earn the income you'd like to earn.

Chapter 8: Trading Breakout Price By Using Strangles And Straddles

In the previous chapter, we looked at the possibility of stock prices remaining within a particular range. We will now examine the reverse scenario that is the case of a stock price that breaks out. The price of a stock could be able to break out either on either side regardless of the direction. This is the great thing about options strategies. They allow us to profit from price fluctuations without having to guess which direction the prices will take.

There are two primary methods that can be employed for this purpose. They are referred to as strangle and strangle. The arrangements are a slightly different, but they serve the same goal. Strangles are more well-known.

Before you set up an exchange like this consider the reason for why you'd want to do it. When we create this type trading, the truth is that the trade could gain profit from the price movement that is a result of rising prices for stocks, or from the movement of declining prices. The nature of price movements isn't crucial. Price movements have to be substantial and therefore we're trying to find a breakout price movement.

This could mean that an important event or news is the best right time to use this strategy. In reality it is possible to apply this strategy four times per year that you can use this kind of strategy to any stock. It is the time the time when quarterly earnings are released. Prices that break into strong breaks occur frequently after earnings calls. The benefit of these methods is that we know that there will be large fluctuations in the price of stocks following earnings calls of companies which are well-known for trading and we do not consider which way the stock is moving in. The announcement of new productions, products or service announcements could cause massive price changes in stocks.

You could also use these strategies to index funds that will alter dramatically as a result of events such as interest rate increases or announcements of GDP growth jobs reports, and other international or political occasions. DIA SPY and SPY can be considered two of the index funds you could employ these strategies.

Straddles and strangles are debits. That is, you purchase them to open these positions, then you sell them in order to close your position, hopefully with profit.

Strangle

A strangle is created with the help of a call and put option to establish a bound range of prices for stocks. However, unlike an iron condor purpose in this instance is to profit when the price of the stock goes away from the boundary we have set up and not to earn a profit in the event that the stock price remains within the bounds of the bounds. The graph below demonstrates that we'll gain money when prices of stocks are not within the two boundaries created by a call option and put option. It's simpler as an iron condor as we'll simply purchase two options to start the trade.

The objective is to make a profit from a significant variation in the price of shares that could be either upwards or downwards. You purchase a call option at a single strike price, which serves as the upper border of the transaction. You then purchase an option to put with a lower strike cost however with the same expiration date. This establishes the lower border of the deal.

The potential profit for strangles is huge. In the ideal scenario, the possibility of profit for the upside is endless. However, in the real world, stock prices do not increase indefinitely. Let's take a look at an example to help you understand possible profits.

If the price of the stock is pushed to the upside the put option expires in vain. The price you that you paid for the put option. If the price of the stock drops down to the downside, the option expires in vain.

The set-up has two breakeven points on both sides that trade. On the other hand the breakeven price represents the strike cost of the option and the premium total paid to purchase both options. On the flip side breakeven points are what the price is of the put, minus the premium total that was paid to purchase both options.

Let's say we own a share of a company trading at $200 a share and we want set up a strangle in advance of the earnings conference. We could purchase an option to call with a strike of $202 at $210. We can purchase put options which has the same expiration dates, but with the strike price of $198 for $205. Our total expense is $415 for the right to participate in the trade.

The breakeven value on the other hand is $198 + $2.05 which is $195.95. If the price of the stock is down, it needs to fall to at least $195.95 before we can earn an income. The breakeven price is $202 x $2.10 = $204.10 which means that the price of the stock must increase at least $204.10 before we can begin earning a profit.

We assume that we purchase the options for 14 days prior to expiration. Let's assume that there's an earnings call scheduled for seven days, so the price action is likely be taking place within 6 days left until expiration. We'll suppose that the price did not move much in the time between.

Six days before expiration, if no other modifications, the put option is now worth

$109 and it is worth $1.12. This means they've lost a significant amount of value. However, prior to earnings calls implied volatility is likely to increase significantly. Therefore, for our purpose we'll assume implied volatility rises up to 45% prior to an earnings call. If this is the case it is priced at $370 and an option to put is at $364. This gives us the total amount of $734. Based on the volatility we could be able to sell it at an profit.

Let's suppose that the earnings conference has some surprises and exceeds expectations. For a $200-a-share stock, an increase in value of $10 or more is not uncommon. Let's assume that it goes up $20 per share in the span of a day. This causes the put option to decrease to $16, which means it's worthless. The call option goes up to $1,810. It is possible to sell it for an incredible profit. This is calculated by subtracting the costs of trading:

$1810 - $415 = $1,395

Let's suppose that the earnings call contains lots of negative news and the stock drops to $170 per share the next morning. If that happens the put option rises in value to $2,800. We make the following profit:

$2800 - $415 = $2,385

As we can know from this that we can make money from stock movements in any direction.

What happens if the price stays within the range? If it does, we'll be losing money on the trade. The most we lose is the cost for the option to purchase. If the price of shares remains between the strike price and its counterpart each option will expire without value.

Straddle

In this article, we'll look at an alternative trade known as the straddle. It is also designed to make money by a breakout towards one side and the opposite. If we are using the straddle, we'll purchase a call option and put option, exactly as we would when we buy strangle. In this instance, however we'll get an identical strike cost and an expiration time of the same date.

The aim of an straddle is the same. We hope to make money from huge price fluctuations and it isn't a matter of what direction the price moves in upwards or downwards is acceptable. If the price is on the upwards, theoretically the maximum gain is infinite. In reality , it's likely to be a fixed amount less the cost needed to purchase each option to open the position. Similar to a strangle, this will be a net loss and therefore you need to purchase options to start this position.

To the negative In theory, the stock could be wiped out of the value it has, however it is a unlikely circumstance. You can still make huge profits from the drop in the price of stocks for example, following an earnings conference.

On the other hand to the upside, the breakeven value is the price at which you strike, plus the total amount that was paid to get into the position. The price of the stock needs to be able to climb at least that amount to begin making profits. On the flip side the breakeven value represents the strike value less amount for the entry into the position. Therefore, if the price of the stock falls, it must be able to drop by at least the amount of making money.

The greatest loss that could be incurred would be incurred if the share price was equal to the strike price that was used. On a graph that shows profits as well as losses, the cross appears to form an X shape that has the bottom being the largest loss at that price.

Let's suppose that we trade Facebook shares at $186 per share. We buy a call put option at-the-money $186 strike price, with 10 days remaining until expiration. If there is a lot of volatility, such as close to an earnings call the price of each option would be around $429. The total cost of entering the trade is $858.

In the next scenario, with five days remaining, Facebook announces their earnings. If the earnings announcement is good news then the price could rise, for example $15 per share. In this scenario the put option is in value as the call is increased to $1532, and we get an income of:

$1532-$858 = $674

If, instead it was a bad news story and the stock plummeted $20 per share The call option would expire useless while the option to put would remain valued at $2004. The total gain will be:

$2004 - $858 = $1,146

The Summary Strangles and Straddles

Strangles and straddles can be bought in order to make open trades. The time to buy the strangle or straddle when you believe that the price of the stock is likely to make a significant movement in either direction however you aren't certain which direction the stock will be moving in. This type of position allows you to not have to guess the direction of the move that the price of your stock. If the outcome is according to your expectations, with the stock experiencing a significant price shift either to the upside or downside, then one your options would expire without value but the other one will rise dramatically which will allow you to make significant profit on the transaction.

Chapter 9: Horizontal Spreads

Horizontal spreads, just like their vertical counterparts are two-legged trades. They're simple to set up, but they can be difficult to understand before entry. This is due to the fact that most horizontal spreads come with the time element that can make them difficult to understand for some. Overall the strategy of horizontal spreads is one that relies on a small amount of luck.

However, the moments you are successful is worth it since the benefits are more when it is done correctly.

Call Calendar Spread

Horizontal spreads can also be known as calendar spreads because of how the two sides of the transaction are set up. The calendar spread called call is best utilized in the first phase of an uptrend, once the trend slows down. The greatest benefit with the spread calendar is you are able to select any time frame you'd like to execute the trade within.

The first part to be established is a long-call position with an expiry date of at minimum 60 days from the date of the trade. The second one is a short-call position with an expiration date of at minimum 30 days. One thing to remember is the fact that the longer call must expire before the short call has expired. The strike costs for both call types are identical.

It is clear the source of the term horizontal calendar originated. Vertical spreads involved placing trades on puts and calls within the same month of expiration but with differing strike price. In this case, we're using the same strike amount, but having different expiration times. This puts the trade in a horizontal direction.

You can set the expiration for the long call that will exceed 60 as well as 90 days. You can also reduce the duration for the short call, too but keep in mind that in the event that you change your mind within the 30-day period the time will decay and you'll get lower premiums upon taking the decision.

Do you need to extend the duration of the call? This is an unwise decision as you'll discover later.

Trade Premise

The principle behind a horizontal spread is basically to enjoy your cake and enjoy it as well. Sometimes, uptrends are slow. As we have seen in earlier chapters, they are lengthy and drawn out, and they can be sideways for extended periods without losing any of their strength. This type of behavior can make a short-term vertical spread inefficient.

Imagine launching an inverse bull call spread, knowing that the price will rise for a long duration, but as time passes by, the price just sits there. While you wait the vertical spread isn't doing anything, and you pay for the privilege of entering the market. It is possible to start an inverse bull put spread, but it's not the best choice to make.

What I am referring to is the fact that if you're aware it is expected to continue for a long period so why limit your profits right at the time of the start? It's not logical. This is why horizontal trading makes more sense, as you will be able to benefit from the sluggishness in the short term as well as the longer term possibility.

In terms of technical analysis it is possible to spot an opportunity in which the presence of counter-trends has increased and intervals last for several weeks at the same time. In these conditions when selling a short-term call (which comes with a shorter expiry date) can help you to capture the price since it will not be able to meet the mark. If price breaks out the range and begins to move up and your long-term call is likely to go to the right direction and you'll be able take advantage of the bull market.

The right strike price in relation to horizontal spreads is more vital than when dealing with vertical spreads. It's not as complicated as it seems. It is essential to examine the resistance levels that are coming up and then choose a price higher than it. Be careful not to pick an amount that is too high. Ideally, you should choose to choose a level that is moderate in strength and that is likely last for at minimum a month.

Utilizing TSLA for an illustration (market cost of $478.15,) let's assume that we want to strike at $500 as the ideal strike amount. A 500 call that expires a day later would cost $28.50. The 500 call that expires in 31 days will earn us an extra $20, resulting in an actual debit transaction that will cost $8.50. The best scenario is the TSLA was to remain under 500 for around a month and then increase it, which would ensure that each leg is operating in a manner that is appropriate.

If the trade does not work as you would like You can change the strategy to suit your needs. Let's say that TSLA appears to be poised to be able to surpass 500 within the coming month. In this case, you can change the trade to an inverse bear call spread. You can also cover the short call and open another that expires in the same month you open the longer call.

In the same way when TSLA falls sharply and it appears as if it's unlikely to surpass 500 any time soon You can alter the trade to an

Bear call spread. It's dependent on how you interpret the current market conditions.

Create Calendar Spread

Horizontal put spreads are comparable in concept to the calendar spread for calls however it aims to profit from the bearish market. Structure of this trade like a call. It's only that you'll buy puts rather than calls. Two legs which are part of the deal.

This leg will be placed at a strike cost that is above an amount of support that is moderate in strength. It has an expiry date which is longer than 30 days but is lower than that of the expiry dates for the longer put leg. It will carry the same strike cost as the short put.

The goal is to reap the advantages of neutrality of the short-term as well as the long term bearishness. The shorter-term, short put offers a higher value, and the long-term put offers capital gains through an increase in intrinsic value when prices drop. It is also an option to trade net debit.

Similar to the calendar spread for calls Put spreads is able to be adjusted according to the kind of market activity observed. The most popular adjustment techniques involve changing it into an upward spread to benefit from price movements.

This concludes our discussion of vertical spread trades. As you will see, they aren't particularly complex and are far simpler to understand and maintain as opposed to vertical spreads. This chapter concludes our examination of spread trades of all types. Spread trades are a step upward from collars, and just like those with collars, can provide solid and long-lasting rewards if properly executed.

Chapter 10: Straddles And Strangles

To conclude our review of options trading strategies, we'll examine strangles and straddles. They're often called combinations trades. This is due to the fact that they require starting legs that include both puts and calls. They're a step up in complexity, but again when you are aware of the fundamentals on the foundation of these trades and you're able to monitor these trades isn't difficult at all.

Let's look at straddles before we do.

Straddles

In contrast to spread trades that tend to be directional, them, the combination trade strategies do not care about how the market will change into. The only thing that is important is the their volatility. In any discussion on these strategies, expect an occasional mention of the so-called 'Greeks which are indicators of volatility, as well as other more sophisticated concepts.

It is possible to do strangles (or strangle) even when you're not the leading expert in the field. The idea behind straddles is simple. It doesn't matter what direction the market moves in the same way as you're concerned about the speed in which it will move.

Each strategy that we've studied so to date have included technical analysis components to the strategies. This means that none of them were solely fundamental in terms of. Combination trades can be made by using only fundamental elements. Events like special occasions macroeconomic announcements, earnings announcements or litigation announcements, and more are a good way to identify potential straddles.

Let's examine how trade is organized.

Trade Structure

The trade is comprised of two parts. The first leg is a long put, which is near the amount and the other is a long call which is also very close to the cash. Because both legs are long you do not have to be concerned about the order that you start your trade's legs. It is crucial to make sure that the expiration dates for each leg are the same.

The ideal scenario is. The fundamentals explode into a flash of volatility, either way. If you have long options that capture both markets, you're in a position to profit regardless of what happens. The concept is that the amount by which prices will change is sufficient to offset any cost you incur to be on the other part of the market.

It creates a zone that is centered around the current market price, which creates a profit-making hurdle for price. So long as price stays within the limits of these there is no chance to earn any profit. So there are two elements that are vital in the straddles. The second is determining the distance you'd like to set up your long-option legs.

The other is to assess whether the level of volatility is expected from the underlying security is a good fit. This can be determined by examining its implied volatility for the an underlying. If it's at or above its historical limits, it is possible to expect significant movements.

The distance that your options strike price match market price? There's a compromise between the volatility and gap between strike prices and the market price in this instance. The lower the risk you can expect the more close the strike prices you will have to be. The closer you go, the greater is the price you have to pay to take the market.

The more expensive the price the greater the minimum price that price must be able to earn profit. It's therefore not necessarily a good idea to get closest to the market price. Let's examine how this is played out by using TSLA as an illustration.

How it works

The market value of TSLA at the moment remains at $478.15. Let's assume that the earnings season is approaching and analysts are divided about what the prospects for TSLA are. There is speculation that should TSLA fails to meet expectations, it will be at risk of losing a larger market share to rivals from the auto industry's mainstream. Some also suggest that should TSLA has a strong growth in earnings that it's a good indicator that the business is on the right track.

If you are in the above situation, you can expect TSLA to either increase in value significantly or drop equally. When directional traders are engaged in figuring out what direction the price is likely to move however, you can take the easy route and just use the strangle.

Let's suppose you select an extended call strike price of $525 and a put strike cost of

$45. For the call, it will cost $15.35 to enter, while the put leg is $11.80. Therefore, the price for trade entry is $27.15. This is the same hurdle that the cost of TSLA must pass in order to turn profits.

Know that there are two obstacles in this case. The first hurdle is that the strike prices pose. The price of the stock has to increase or decrease to the minimum at which the prices are set before you start thinking about potential profits. In the next step, the premium needs to increase by at minimum $27.15 before you can earn a profits in the financial sense. In this scenario the increase in the intrinsic value must guarantee that the premium will surpass the financial threshold if one option becomes cash-flow positive.

When it comes to expiry dates, as far as they are concerned, you can select either the current month or the month following. Because the options set to expire the month that follows will contain the full time value so you'll pay more for the options. So, it's best to utilize time decay in your favor and purchase the month-to-month options.

Strangles

Once you've figured out the workings of straddles now is the time to take an in-depth review of strangles. I'm calling them short because they follow the same method like the straddles. The difference is that the options strike prices are more distant in anticipation of a greater risk than the strangle.

Both trades share the identical number of legs them , and both rely on the same rules when setting up. If you know one, the other won't cause any problems.

Chapter 11: Risk Management

In contrast to directional trading, risk management isn't as important in trading options. It doesn't mean that it's irrelevant. In fact, it isn't. The difference is that although risk management takes on a strong quantitative component in relation to trades that are directional but in the case of options, it's more qualitative. There are however some minor quantitative elements you need to know about.

Risk Numbers

The most important and first risk factor to be aware of is the risks per transaction. This is the same as the highest risk you are taking when you make an option trade. Keep in mind that when you alter the trading in secondary settings, you must be sure to stay within your risk limit for these situations as well.

What are your limits on risk? They are usually expressed as one number that represents the proportion of your account that you're putting at risk per trade. Keep in mind that you're not likely be able to win every trade you make. If you're putting 10 percent of your account's balance on one trade only to lose 10 trades in the same row, you've declared yourself bankrupt.

This decrease in size of the account is called drawing down. It is generally recommended to try to achieve a monthly drawdown that is not more than 4 percent while trading options. That means that if you lose more than 4 percent of your account in the course of a month, you must put your trading down and stop for a while. Many traders face major issues with this because they believe that a day off is a wasted day.

It's true that it is essential to trade on days that you're performing at your peak to the greatest extent you can. This will make sure that your results will be as efficient as they could be. Making sure you're performing the best you can be means that you'll have to record your physical and mental state by keeping a diary.

The journal you keep for trading should keep record of any information related to trades you've made, along with any screens of the market that you could have viewed it during the entry and exit.

Overall, make sure that you don't risk more than 2percent of your account for each trade and be sure to stop trading when you reach the monthly drawdown limit. If you follow these two aspects from a mathematical perspective and you'll be fine.

Qualitative Aspects

The monitoring of your mental and physical health is vital in order to become an effective trader. That means you'll be required to follow a few basic methods to make sure you're in the best condition you can be. A few of the tips below might appear to be common sense but you'll be shocked by how easy to overlook the tips are by beginners to trading.

The reason is the fact that trading is an exciting and exciting venture which is meant to keep you entertained for the duration of time and make you feel stressed. However, it can make you feel stressed when you get it wrong. In reality it is, when done correctly trading can be a rather boring task. This is a great thing.

Exercise

Never ignore your physical health. Trading is a mind-based activity however that doesn't mean you have to ignore your body. The benefits of exercising are numerous, and in this moment, it's normal to exercise. No matter what type of exercise you do the act of moving is enough to bring you into an improved state of mind.

Make it a point to plan the time to exercise. If you're feeling tired or sick, don't make a trade.

Diet

Diet is the second major element for our overall health. It is important to eat well and eat a balanced diet. Don't skip meals in order for trading and don't consume a large meal prior to studying the market. The most important thing you do not would like to do is be tired when you do this.

Lifestyle

Do you plan to be out until odd hours in the evening and then to trade profitably at 6A.M the next morning? It's not that you have to be monks in order to make money , but consistency and discipline are vital. It is not possible to trade when you are drunk or even worse. If you have too many people that cause you to continually be angry about certain things that happen in your life, you will not be able to trade effectively. You should take some time to sort things out and then get back to market.

Journal

Keep track of your moods in the form of your trading records. What was your mood when you made an exchange? It is important to reflect on your trading decisions towards the close of each week. Also, make time to work on your skills. Develop a schedule and follow the rules strictly.

This is, after all, your business of trading!

Chapter 12: Fundamental Analysis

We're about to begin diving into the trading options market even though it doesn't appear to be. The first step to trading options with success is to to determine the right ones to engage in. So how do you plan to determine the best options for you to participate in.

There are two ways to go about this. The one is the fundamental analysis, which is the subject this chapter is going to cover. The second one is technical analysis and will be the topic of the following chapter will discuss. As I stated in the past, many traders divide themselves into groups in regards to the different approaches and choose one method and avoid the other.

This is a simple way of thinking about things. The reality is that you have to mix one with another. The extent of this is based on the level of comfort you have. There isn't a single "right" way to analyze the market. If you're a person who is an approach that is solely technical, that's fine. This simply means that it's the best for you, not the only way to approach things.

After all that, let's dive into the basic analysis.

Fundamentals

It could take several volumes to provide fundamental analysis in all its aspects. This is due to the fact that at its the core, fundamental analysis is designed to determine what a company's worth. It is based on the idea that stocks are part of a larger business and to comprehend what it is expected to accomplish, you have to be aware of the business and how it functions.

As you're able to imagine that a lot is subjective since there aren't any set standards for what a "great" company is. One could argue that all successful businesses earn profits, but factors such as profit margins and management quality can have a significant effect on bottom-line. For instance, Apple makes more money than Walmart however does that indicate that it is a bad company?

In any case, our objective in trading options isn't to understand the inner workings of the business completely. Keep in mind that we're trying to look for opportunities that can be seized upon. When we spot an opportunity, it is important in a position to look at the financials of the company concerned and determine if it's suitable for any of our strategies. Where do we start?

Reading

It's not a revolutionary idea to say that, but to make an analysis that is fundamentally sound for your needs, you'll need to read. A number of times. The Wall Street Journal isn't going to be enough It's best to join newsletters that aren't widely known as well as visit websites like Seeking Alpha and Valuewalk. These are the more popular ones. A large number of basic traders make their job easier by focusing their attention on one particular sector and limiting their focus.

This is an excellent strategy because the opportunities are all over the world. Be aware that strategies for options are diverse therefore it's not as if you won't be capable of maximizing the opportunities that are available in the particular industry. If you believe you'd prefer to invest in tech firms, then do it. If women's lingerie inspires you, then do it and concentrate on those businesses exclusively. It's your choice.

An important step before calculating any figures is to get an understanding of the area or industry in general. Select something that is easy to grasp. For instance, Facebook might be a appealing stock to invest in however if you're not a fan of the site and don't know much about the driving forces of the technology industry, there's not any point in trying to learn about the foundations of Facebook.

It's better choosing a sector or sector model you like the most. Technology, for instance, might be too complicated for you however, what is the non-alcoholic beverage sector? Some of the companies that operate in this area comprise Coca Cola, Pepsi, Monster, Red Bull etc. If you decide to expand into alcohol-based drinks, the list becomes more extensive.

The point is to not consider yourself to become able to grasp of everything at all. Begin with the things that you believe you know and don't have the desire to be an expert in everything. Once you've narrowed those industries that you think that you understand fairly well It's time to increase your attention.

Making Connections with them

Find out all the information you can find on companies that are in the sector you prefer. If you prefer to focus on just a few companies within that particular industry, then do it. In any case, you should get to understand them better. If you're overwhelmed by the number of firms in the industry or field you've selected, try to narrow your search to a smaller size.

Understanding your company of interest is about discovering what their character is similar to. It may seem strange, however every business has its own distinct character which is evident in their way of conducting business. Coca Cola's method of marketing its brand is distinct from that of Pepsi is doing, as an instance. When you look at the automobile business, the way Mercedes-Benz promotes its vehicles is different from what its major rivals, Audi and BMW, are doing.

One way to determine this is to look at their management and their philosophies in relation to the field they're operating in. Staying in the automobile business, Mercedes invests heavily into the most niche sports with high tech such for Formula One whereas Audi sticks to the same high tech however, different sports like the World Endurance Racing by way of its subsidiary companies (Szymkowski 2017). BMW does not compete in any racing series at the time of this writing.

These decisions all flow from the management, and making use of Google or Twitter to learn about their philosophy is fairly simple these days. Don't be relying too heavily on the opinions of analysts in this moment, but do take an examination of what the essence of financial news. Through this process, you'll also learn the historical background of the companies that you are interested in. With this information at hand, you can proceed on to the next phase.

I'd like to highlight an exception to this procedure. In the next chapter you'll learn strategies to capitalize on the potential for extreme volatility in a specific stock. If you want to identify such stocks rather than trying to break the search to a specific sector, and based on your ability to grasp them, you could search the media for information about lawsuits, settlementsand patents that are awaiting approval or class action lawsuit outcomes and other such things.

Another thing you could look for are restructuring announcements or earnings announcements by a big firm following a string of disappointing quarters. Because of the magnitude of the business concerned it is likely to raise prices significantly upon receiving positive news, or lower prices a lot when it receives negative information. If you are able to find companies that can be a good fit for volatility strategies, you can immediately move into the following step.

Financials

If you are thinking of investing in a business for the long-term that's at which the first chapter of the fundamentals book will start. It is, however, not our aim and our job is much less complicated. But it is still necessary to perform the effort. There's no limit to the financial ratios that you can utilize to assess a business. In this article I'll show you the top ratios and methods to gain a better understanding of the financials of a business.

When trading options for a company the most important thing to know from a financial standpoint is what's occurring that could disrupt your strategies. For instance there is something that appears to be off, or is there an other problem that could make the stock behave in ways that are harmful to your plans. The objective is not to determine if it's a good company or not. That's not the issue.

It's a simple enough task to remember, but with the vast amount of information you can collect for companies, it's not difficult to lose yourself trying to determine if it was the right decision in opening an entirely new facility in nothing inside the Amazonian jungle. Here are some of the essential aspects you must examine and consider when taking a look at the financial side of things:

Ratio of Total Capital to Debt It is often expressed in percentages too. It's that the amount total of debt is divided by total of equity and debt. It is possible to get these two numbers by looking at the balance sheet that will show the total amount of debt and also the equity total (which is at the lower left.)

Companies with large amounts of debt don't necessarily mean they're bad. They may be problematic from a long-term financial perspective, but that's not our goal here. The reality is that companies' stocks generally tend to have higher volatility. Therefore, if you see an organization that's been in the news or is awaiting a verdict of any kind and has more than 70 to 80 percent of its debt as capital base is, you can be sure that the stock is likely to go up in a specific direction.

Companies that have lower levels of debt tend to be better able to withstand the rigors of time and are less unstable. If you are looking for stocks that are more predictable in their manner, you may be able to identify opportunities on this indicator. Aside from that What is the reason why the levels of debt affect volatility in stocks so much? It has to do with leverage. have to do with leverage. Debt is the amount a company has borrowed to increases their return on successful ventures. This is evidenced in the equity that is nothing more than the price of stock.

Do you remember making 100% returns for only one percent by with leverage in the case we examined in the previous section? The same principle applies at a higher level in this case.

Ratio between Price and Earnings

Also known as the P/E rate This refers to the ratio of price divided by earning per share. The number does not matter in and of itself, but it's compared against the ratios used by other companies within its sector. For instance, if company A has 60 P/E however the other companies in the sector are selling at 20 per cent which is obviously, there's something wrong.

Do you think this is a good thing or bad issue? It all is dependent on the approach you're trying to implement. The first thing to take a look at is the length of time you keep your position. The rule of thumb is that options must be kept for at minimum a month. In the event that the company appears to be overvalued and is it possible that, based on the conversations around it that the market will cause prices to fall? If yes, then do you consider a short-term strategy?

This is the point where fundamental analysis is more of an art rather than it is a science. If you think the market will cause prices to fall You could seek evidence on the technical aspect of things. You'll find out during the following chapter. If both forms of analysis are saying the exact same issue (that declines are inevitable) and you're in a position to take the short-term strategy could be the most effective option.

You could also discover that nothing is that is unusual. That's acceptable too. It's not the intention to search for skeletons hidden in the closet. You're trying to get an understanding of the situation. Most of the time, you will not find anything that is alarming. If you employ your P/E ratio as a criterion for screening then you should look for companies selling at multiples significantly higher than the rest of the firms in the field.

There are also businesses that are trading at less than the other companies in their respective industries. It is important to understand the reason for this in both instances and whether repricing is likely within your time frame for holding. If all of the above factors match then taking a position is logical.

Free Cash Flow

Cash flow free is a crucial indicator to monitor when you're considering investing in a company over long-term. Since we're trying to explore its possibilities it doesn't be as important for us. However, there's something we can learn from looking at the subject.

The easiest method to gauge the level of financial strength a business's financials is to first glance at the price-to-free cash flow multiplier and examine it against that of the PE ratio. In most cases, you'll notice that the former will be higher than the latter. This isn't bad in and of itself.

But, a significant discrepancy can indicate a number of issues in particular if the discrepancy has existed for more than five years. The reason behind this conclusion is at the heart of the concept of free cash flow in the first place. The name implies that it is money leftover, or free when all expenditures have been paid.

I'm not interested in getting into accounting details, however there are certain non-cash expenses that are taken out of the bottom line of a business (income) and other costs that can be altered to increase revenue. Therefore the income statement reveals the expenses of a business and its bottom line after subtracting from the income.

The cash flow report shows how much cash flows into. The income does not necessarily equal the cash. A business could make huge profits, but they are only on paper. The cash flow report shows the percentage of the income was in cold hard cash. A paper piece isn't enough to pay for your company's obligations. It's cash that pays this, so be aware of it.

Free cash flow incorporates a highly crucial aspect, which is capital expenses, also known as capex. Capex is the amount of money used to create more assets for the business and does not subtract from the revenue. Businesses that are involved in the infrastructure or machinery industries or expanding usually have large capex numbers which subtract cash flow.

In the end, you'll see your the flow of cash and income differ significantly. This isn't cause for concern, however it must be examined. What is the exact purpose of this money being used for? If a company is constantly high capex, is it benefitting from that investment or is the business consistently making poor investments?

The annual report can provide you with the specifics of this , however, there's an easier method to assess the quality of investment in capex. The revenue should grow by a significant amount over time, and so should your cash flow (which is within the flow report.) If you don't see any of these two things happening, then examine if it is a unique scenario. But, you must be looking for an opportunity now and begin asking your self what strategy could work best for this particular company.

Because of its fragile situation, a bearish approach may work, however, betting on fundamentals isn't a good idea. The reason is that investors don't want to see their stocks fall. It's a matter of human nature. So, in these situations it's recommended to look at charts from a technical perspective and try at shorting the stock in resistance zones (you'll discover what they are in the following chapter.)

What happens if you discover the perfect stock with a high free cash flow, but due to some reason, it has slowed earnings? It's like finding a treasure in the sand, to be truthful. It is worth buying this stock in the long term and employ strategies like the covered call that will yield you income on the investment.

I'd like to point out that certain options strategies require the taking of what could appear as a short-term position in the stock, but in actual they're an expression of optimism for the long-term. Since you don't have any strategies yet I'm sure this may be unclear. My suggestion is to be aware that your responsibility is to comprehend the fundamentals of the strategy for options that you'll learn from this book, and not focusing on the direction in which positions are taken.

A lot of options traders categorize strategies as either bearish or bullish, but don't think about figuring out the meaning of what the method actually implying. This is my goal to keep the possibility of making this mistake.

In any case whether you do it in a way, looking at free cash flow in relation to revenue, as well as the price-to-value ratio to each of these measures can help you determine where your company is relative quickly. You can also compare cost and free flow rates with those of its competitors in the same industry. Similar to the P/E, If you notice huge discrepancies and you want to investigate further to determine the reason behind it.

Insider Trading Disclosures

The SEC is a major regulator of the stock market , and the chance of a senior manager of a publicly traded company trying to sell off company stock and then hyping about it is very unlikely in the present. However, the disclosures made to insider traders will give you an idea of who is the owner of what percentage of the company.

The form to be looking for is the 13-F disclosure. If significant changes in ownership occur or when existing groups of major owners of stock alter their ownership They will have to make a disclosure on 13-F. They are delayed by a month, which means they're not really time. Nowadays, you'll find that the majority of public companies are owned by institutions , such as index funds or mutual funds.

So, you'll see many 13-Fs from these companies and you might believe that they are running away from the market by selling their stakes in it or by buying it in the expectation of huge market bullishness. Although this may be true in some instances, you need to know how mutual funds as well as index funds operate with their own rules to adhere to. The manager of mutual funds has one of the most difficult jobs on the market.

They must adhere to very strict guidelines when managing their money (McGowan 2019). It is essential to concentrate on specific areas, businesses of the same size and must not invest more than a predetermined limit within a single company. If any of these rules are broken, they have to change their portfolios. In addition to this, they must also be able to earn some money. It's similar to me saying that you must keep driving at 60 MPH within the middle of the lane, and reach your destination within an amount that is set and push the accelerator no more than half way down. It could get quite intense.

Index funds don't face such an issue, however they must rebalance their portfolios. They also have strict limits on investments on stocks in particular, and once the limits are reached and they have to adjust their portfolios. The majority of 13-Fs that you will see are the result of this rebalancingprocess, particularly in the case of businesses that are owned by institutions.

The form 13-F can be obtained simple enough. It is no cost by the SEC through the EDGAR database. Additionally, the companies themselves release relevant announcements about ownership structures as they occur. Your job is to gather an understanding of the identity of the organizations that own the business.

In particular, you must examine the hedge funds which control the company. There are plenty of activist hedge funds which scour the market looking for opportunities that they can get involved and generate value by making some adjustments. If you come across one of these hedge funds with an excellent reputation and has a substantial ownership stake, either through the news or in the 13-F, it is likely that it will change.

However, it doesn't mean that volatility is likely. It could take some time or it could require a couple of years. There's no method to know this, however, looking through the reports and news from the company can assist you in understanding the situation. There could be a situation in which the current management is fighting against the hedge fund, and there's a huge shareholder vote set to take place that could affect the stock in any direction, as an example.

Certain hedge funds perform something different and it can be difficult to discern what's going on and what their investment strategy is. You can determine this more easily by listening to recordings of the analyst call which follow earnings announcements. These calls are the time when Wall Street investment analysts who are closely following the company have questions for the management.

The typical Wall Street analyst isn't the most reliable source of information this instance because so much of their connection to the business is based on how positive they portray the situation. It is nevertheless instructive to listen to calls. Be careful not to get caught up believing that everything is going well. If there's a substantial hedge fund stake in the ownership, the chief director of the hedge fund firm will be on the conference call too and then the fireworks will begin to erupt. If the ownership is on good relations with the fund manager , and If there's no shady activity happening, the situation will be in good stead of being amicable.

A well-known instance of an earnings call that alerted markets that there was something off was when the managing director at the hedge fund Greenlight Capital, David Einhorn asked an ex-CFO at Lehman Brothers, Erin Callan regarding discrepancies in the income and cash flow statement that Lehman Brothers Wall Street giant had filed in the early part of the year 2008 (La Roche, 2012). Callan denied any false statements, however, it was revealed that she didn't know about what was happening within her own business. Lehman

Brothers went bankrupt within several months after that phone call.

Pay attention to earnings calls. They'll be optimistic and romantic however, if there's anything suspicious , it could be the victim of questions that will be asked in these calls.

Sentiment Analysis

Sentiment analysis is about understanding what the market as a whole is doing and the current consensus on what direction the market will move. It's not necessarily limited to one particular company or stock. It's true that you might find that hidden secret that could increase in value, however if the general market conditions are negative then it's not going to move anywhere. It's the way it operates.

There are some numbers that you can use to determine the mood of the market. Let's take a look in greater detail.

Implied Volatility

Implied volatility, or IV as it's referred to is an indicator of the extent to which the price is likely to change in the near term as a result of any stimuli (McGowan 2019, 2019). The higher the number the higher the likelihood of a change. IV is distinct from historical volatility, which is the level of volatility in the past like the name implies.

If you notice a high IV number, this indicates that the market is predicting a massive change is in the horizon in either direction. Most often, you'll see IV numbers rise ahead of an announcement on news or any other major factor that could affect the market.

Open Interest

Open interest is the quantity of options contracts currently trading in any stock. It is a fact that many novices are unaware of the importance that open interest has. This figure indicates the existence of an increase in participation from the public . Therefore If you observe an increase in the amount of contracts and contracts, you can be certain that the current trend will likely come close to a conclusion.

In the course of a bullish trend for a long time, you'll see the number of calls that are available to trade increase steadily in response to the growing demand from the general population. The interest in calls is peak as the trend is about to close. In the same way, you can expect increases in puts just prior to the end of a bearish trend.

The number you track will give you an idea of how the most intelligent investment is up to.

VIX

The Volatility Index or VIX is one of the most closely observed indices of the market for stocks. The index itself comes by the VI of SPX options (McGowan 2019, 2019). IV is a reference to implied volatility, as you've just discovered, and SPX is for the index which is a representation of the S&P500 index of the stock market that is the market's broad index that reflects the performance in 500 most powerful stocks that are trading in America at the moment.

So as such, the VIX gives a fairly accurate view of the SPX but it could be used to determine the general market's mood is. It is a good indicator of market sentiment. VIX tends to grow in value when fears are high (bearishness anticipated) and fall with optimism high (bullishness anticipated.) It doesn't mean that every high or low is a sign of something. But If you spot the VIX hitting a new high and you're considering taking advantage of an investment that is long You might want to rethink your plan.

Ratio of Call/Put

The name implies that this number represents an indication of the amount of calls and puts that are in the stock. The opinions are divided on the actual value the significance of this number. It is a sign of what other traders think about the stock. But should you consider rethinking your investment should you find yourself going in the opposite direction?

Conclusion

We are now at the conclusion of this guide. We began by examining the basics of market and the way price is displayed on the form of a chart. Keep in mind that you can employ candlestick price forms to further confirm the entry point to your strategies.

If, for instance, you are planning to use an option to trade a bear call spread and you see an elongated pin bar near the level of major resistance is a reliable indicator that the price is about to go through a downward slide. Any candlestick pattern that you intend to trade should be supported by a suitable price context. For example, seeing pin bars within a narrow range, or with a slight sideways move during a huge upward trend is not a good indicator.

Although figuring out price environments can be difficult it is possible to start by trading ranges. They tend to be steady and their lateral movement guarantees that the price won't elude you like when you trade in the case of trends. Trends are the best way to earn the highest returns Of course, however finding a trend the right moment is not easy and most of the time the entry you make is not optimal.

Options eliminate this issue due to their fact that they have to select strike prices and not entry levels like with trading directional options. Start with a range and proceed to. The ability to discern trends from ranges is worthless if you don't manage risk effectively.

The most accurate measurement in risk control is the consistency and that requires a variety of things, but most of all, discipline. It requires discipline to adhere to the risk limits you set for each trade and avoid falling to the temptation of increasing the risk per trade in pursuit of possible profits. We've observed how your math for profit margins can get distorted when you're not consistent in this area.

Your attitude could be the cause if you have trouble staying in a state of mind. Many of us are raised with negative notions of success and money, and at times, it's easy to consider money to be the sole way to be happy. It puts us into a difficult situation when we have to take losses, which are the case in trading, and put our minds in an "all or none" type of thinking that is normal in academics as well as typical job situations.

Trading isn't your typical setting, and therefore needs to be considered an actual business. It is important to know the way that odds work, and if you continue to understand the basics of how odds work, however you still feel angry over some losses in trades, then your mind is to blame.

In the final section, we have discussed four profit-making options trading strategies that you can use right now. The covered call and collar are both market neutral strategies that will bring you a substantial amount of income each month. In the next step, consider applying the strategies to spread calls as described in the last chapter.

There are many combinations you can play with in relation to strike price, so be aware of this when choosing the strike prices.

It is essential to become a successful trader. Therefore, make sure that you always practice your skills in understanding S/R levels and markets. Practice and you'll reach your goals.

Thank you thank you for the opportunity to go through this book. I'm sure it will help you trade more effectively and, most importantly, teach you how to earn instant money, nearly completely risk-free.

www.ingramcontent.com/pod-product-compliance
Lightning Source LLC
Chambersburg PA
CBHW050407120526
44590CB00015B/1866